VATICAN CITY

TITLES IN THE MODERN NATIONS OF THE WORLD SERIES INCLUDE:

Afghanistan	Kenya
Algeria	Kuwait
Argentina	Lebanon
Australia	Liberia
Austria	Libya
Belize	Mexico
Bolivia	Morocco
Brazil	Nicaragua
Cambodia	Nigeria
Canada	North Korea
Chile	Pakistan
China	Panama
Colombia	Peru
Congo	Philippines
Costa Rica	Poland
Cuba	Russia
Czech Republic	Saudi Arabia
Denmark	Scotland
Egypt	Somalia
England	South Africa
Ethiopia	South Korea
Finland	Spain
France	Sri Lanka
Germany	Sudan
Greece	Sweden
Guatemala	Switzerland
Haiti	Syria
Hungary	Taiwan
India	Thailand
Indonesia	Turkey
Iran	United Arab Emirates
Iraq	United States
Ireland	Vatican City
Israel	Vietnam
Italy	Yemen
Japan	
Jordan	

VATICAN CITY

BY MARTHA CAPWELL FOX

LUCENT BOOKS

An imprint of Thomson Gale, a part of The Thomson Corporation

THOMSON

GALE

Detroit • New York • San Francisco • San Diego • New Haven, Conn. • Waterville, Maine • London • Munich

THOMSON
—————✴—————™
GALE

945.634 CAP

Fox, Martha Capwell.
Vatican City.

© 2006 Thomson Gale, a part of The Thomson Corporation.

Thomson and Star Logo are trademarks and Gale and Lucent Books are registered trademarks used herein under license.

For more information, contact
Lucent Books
27500 Drake Rd.
Farmington Hills, MI 48331-3535
Or you can visit our Internet site at http://www.gale.com

LIBRARY OF CONGRESS CATALOGING-IN-PUBLICATION DATA

Fox, Martha Capwell.
 Vatican City / by Martha Capwell Fox.
   p. cm. — (Modern nations of the world)
 Includes bibliographical references.
 ISBN 1-59018-733-4 (hard cover : alk. paper)
 1. Vatican City—Juvenile literature. I. Title. II. Series.
DG800.F68 2005
945.6'34—dc22
                                                          2005015309

Printed in the United States of America

CONTENTS

INTRODUCTION

UNIQUE AMONG NATIONS

The State of the City of the Vatican, to use its official name, is the world's smallest sovereign nation. It covers less than 109 acres, making it less than half the size of New York's Central Park. Vatican City is entirely surrounded by the city of Rome. Two miles (3.2km) of walls mark most of its boundaries, though at the edge of St. Peter's Square, the border is nothing more than a line of stones in the plaza.

In addition to the area behind its walls, the Vatican's territory includes thirteen other churches, basilicas, and buildings in Rome, such as St. John Lateran (the actual cathedral of the diocese of Rome, of which the pope is bishop), St. Mary Major, the San Callisto palace, and the pope's summer residence outside the city, Castel Gandolfo.

Vatican City has about 925 citizens in residence, making it the smallest nation in terms of population as well as size. Most of them are ordained men who hold high offices in the Curia, the governing bureaucracy of the Catholic Church. However, there are also ordinary priests, a handful of nuns, some laypeople, and the soldiers of the papal army, the Swiss Guard and their families, among the Vatican's citizens. Formerly, most Vatican citizens were Italian born; since the reign of John XXIII (1958–1963), however, American, Latin American, African, and Asian bishops and cardinals, as well as many from other European nations, have held Vatican passports. Vatican citizenship is conferred when one takes up a post; it ends when the job (or the jobholder's life) ends.

This cosmopolitan group goes about its day-to-day work speaking in Italian, though French and English are commonly spoken as well. Nevertheless, Latin remains the official language of the Vatican, and all documents are promulgated in the ancient tongue, as well as in modern languages.

As a secular nation, Vatican City issues its own coins, license plates, and postage stamps. Economically, it is self-supporting. Citizens pay no taxes, but the income from visitors to the

Vatican Museums is more than enough to meet the budget for mundane things like building maintenance and streetlights.

A UNIQUE POLITICAL ENTITY

Vatican City is unique on the roster of nations. It is the only theocracy (a nation whose laws are based on religious rules) in the world with an elected monarch, in this case, the pope. Another anomaly is that most of the electorate—the members of the College of Cardinals who are under the age of eighty—are neither citizens nor residents of Vatican City, though they are considered the "princes" of the Catholic Church. It is also the only political entity in the world in which the ruler, the pope, is an elected absolute monarch, as well as the spiritual leader of a religion, in this case the Roman Catholic Church.

The Vatican's exceptional clout in world affairs springs partly from the pope's authority in matters of faith over a vast number of people. Sixteen percent of the world's inhabitants —an estimated 1.1 billion people—are baptized Roman Catholics, members of the largest single religious denomination on earth. This allows the Roman Catholic Church to influence the public and political affairs of many nations to a certain degree through its faithful. The Vatican's reach across virtually every national border in the world allows it to exert its will in ways that are the envy of ordinary nations, even the most powerful ones. Modern popes, particularly John Paul II (1978–2005), have not hesitated to encourage their flock to vote and otherwise influence public policies in their own countries in ways that are consistent with Catholic teaching. Further influence is wielded by the highly respected diplomatic corps of the Holy See, which represents

Members of the Swiss Guard, the 100-man papal army, stand watch over Vatican City.

Pope Benedict XVI blesses pilgrims at the end of his inaugural Mass in St. Peter's Square in April 2005.

the pope and the Catholic Church in 174 countries, and dozens of international policy-making organizations.

SEE THE DIFFERENCE?

In the finely parsed language of international and diplomatic law, Vatican City and the Holy See are not one and the same. The State of the City of the Vatican is the territory where the Holy See is located. The Holy See of Rome, to use its full title, is the Roman Catholic diocese of Rome. (*See* is another word for "diocese.") The bishop of Rome—the pope—has been recognized as the head of the Church, and the first among bishops, for most of the Church's history.

Vatican City was created in 1929 by an agreement, known as the Lateran Treaty, between the Church and the Italian government. Vatican City's political function is to oversee and conduct the work of the Church's properties in Rome as a sovereign, independent entity. The Vatican owes its existence to concessions made by both the Holy See and the Italian government. Italy agreed to recognize the pope as a sovereign leader and to guarantee his safety and the ability of the Church to act as an independent entity. In return, the pope and Church agreed to relinquish any claims to Italian territory other than Vatican City.

The Holy See is the actual government of the Roman Catholic Church. Its authority is not tied to a place; in theory, the pope could rule from anywhere he wanted. If Vatican City were destroyed or taken over by a hostile power which expelled the pope (which has happened several times in history), the Holy See would still exist. It is the Holy See, rather than Vatican City, that is the international entity, with the power to conclude treaties with nations and to send and receive diplomats. Though technically the Vatican and the Holy See are separate entities, in everyday usage the terms are interchangeable.

The Vatican is many things to many people. To many national and international leaders and diplomats, the Vatican is both a center of influence and a facilitator of quiet but effective behind-the-scenes diplomacy. To people who study painting, sculpture, and architecture or who simply love the arts, the Vatican is the greatest museum in the world. To Romans who make their living in the hospitality industry, the Vatican, with its millions of visitors a year, is a gold mine. To Christians, and especially Roman Catholics, it is one of the most sacred places in the world, and, through the presence of the pope, the source of spiritual guidance and leadership of their Church.

THE GREATEST
MUSEUM IN
THE WORLD

1

Vatican City is a treasure trove of art and architecture. It is the only entire nation to be declared a World Heritage Site by the United Nations (UN). Thousands of works by the most brilliant Western painters, sculptors, and architects, from ancient Greeks and Romans to twentieth century artists, are found here. Even dim bureaucratic hallways and humble back staircases boast magnificent murals, complex tapestries, and exquisite sculptures. It has been said that to see every precious object in the Vatican would take years.

Vatican City houses a significant portion of the world's most extraordinary art because the Church was the biggest customer for art in Europe in the centuries between the fall of the Roman Empire in the fifth century and the start of the eighteenth century. When few people could read, sculptures, frescoes, paintings, and stained glass windows served to teach piety and preach the faith. To the popes, the faithful, and particularly the artists, it was only natural that the most beautiful attempts to portray the relationship between God and humanity should be created for the Vatican.

The collaboration between pontiffs and artists reached its zenith in the Renaissance. Popes Nicholas V (1447–1455) and Julius II (1503–1513) are credited with transforming the Vatican from a run-down medieval cathedral and its environs into the monumental basilica and museums of today.

ST. PETER'S BASILICA
The largest church in the world, St. Peter's Basilica stands over a site that Christians have revered for centuries as the burial place of the first pope, Simon Peter (died ca. A.D. 66), the leader of the apostles. Inscribed in Latin in large gold

11

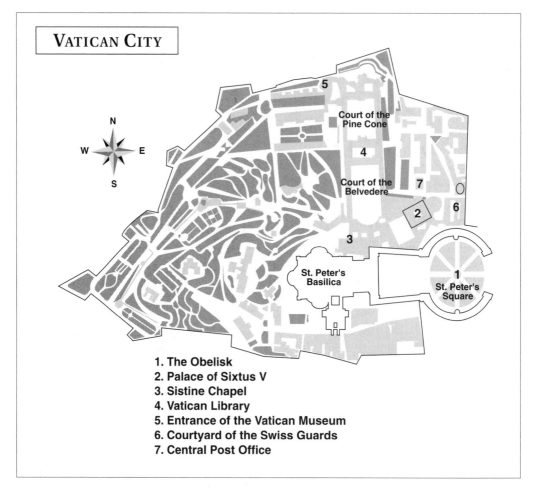

VATICAN CITY

Court of the
Pine Cone

Court of the
Belvedere

St. Peter's
Basilica

St. Peter's
Square

1. **The Obelisk**
2. **Palace of Sixtus V**
3. **Sistine Chapel**
4. **Vatican Library**
5. **Entrance of the Vatican Museum**
6. **Courtyard of the Swiss Guards**
7. **Central Post Office**

mosaic letters around the inside of the great dome of the church are Jesus's words to Peter, as recorded in the Gospel of Matthew: *Tu es Petrus et super hanc petra aedificabo Ecclesiam meam* ("You are Peter, and upon this rock I will build my church"). Roman Catholics regard these words as Christ's commissioning of Peter as the first pope.

Ironically, this great sacred site was originally the location of a Roman circus, an arena where athletic competitions and races were held. Circuses were free entertainment for the people of Rome, and during the persecutions of the first three centuries A.D., the entertainment sometimes included executing Christians in various grisly ways.

According to tradition, supported to a degree by archaeological evidence, Peter was crucified upside down in the circus, near the obelisk, and was buried in a large cemetery adjacent to it. The spot believed to be his tomb is now beneath the main altar of St. Peter's.

"Old" Saint Peter's

The first great church on this site was built circa A.D. 320 by Constantine, the first Roman emperor to convert to Christianity. Ancient accounts describe a magnificent space, 208 feet (63.4m) by 355 feet (108.2m), its roof 110 feet (33.5m) above the floor, resplendent in gold, mosaics, and art. Constantine's church both destroyed the Roman cemetery that had stood on top of Vatican Hill for three hundred years and contributed to its preservation, because he had the mausoleums unroofed and filled with dirt, and then constructed the church over them. Though the original burial places seemingly disappeared, under the basilica they were protected from centuries of weather and danger.

Is This Peter?

For sixteen centuries, believers had only their faith to bolster their conviction that the earthly remains of Simon Peter the Galilean fisherman, the first pope, rested in the grotto below the basilica's main altar.

Then, in 1939, Pope Pius XI was buried there, alongside several of his predecessors. Work began shortly thereafter on converting the grotto to an underground chapel. Workers soon uncovered Roman graves, with both Christian and pagan symbols. Then a red-painted wall, mentioned in ancient accounts of Peter's shrine, was uncovered. The workers came out, and a team of Jesuit archaeologists went in. On December 23, 1950, Pope Pius XII announced that Peter's tomb had been found.

Had Peter himself been found? Papal pronouncement on that had to wait until 1968. Laboratory analysis of bones found near the red wall concluded that they were those of a robust man who died in his sixties—which could describe Peter. Convinced, Paul VI announced that Peter's remains had been identified. Though not every archaeologist or theologian was equally sure, Paul VI had the bones returned to the grotto, where they can be seen behind glass today.

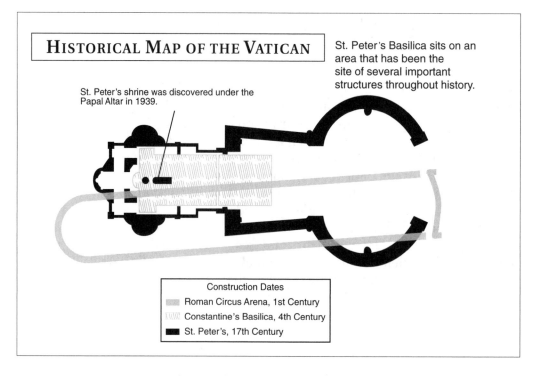

HISTORICAL MAP OF THE VATICAN

St. Peter's Basilica sits on an area that has been the site of several important structures throughout history.

St. Peter's shrine was discovered under the Papal Altar in 1939.

Construction Dates
Roman Circus Arena, 1st Century
Constantine's Basilica, 4th Century
St. Peter's, 17th Century

This church stood for twelve hundred years, gradually being filled to overflowing with medieval altars and tombs. The decades when the popes resided in Avignon in France contributed to the neglect of the building, and in 1450, Pope Nicholas V decided to replace the old church with a larger, newer basilica.

BUILDING A BASILICA

This newer basilica was a monumental effort that took 176 years. The cross-shaped design with four huge piers supporting a grand dome was approved by Pope Julius II in the early sixteenth century; however, most of the work of building the new cathedral was not carried out until Pope Paul III named the great sculptor Michelangelo Buonarroti as the architect in 1546. Michelangelo retained most of the original classical Greek and Roman designs for the church. But he scrapped the plans for the dome and replaced it with a daring structure, 137 feet (41.7m) in diameter, which would tower 435 feet (132.5m) above the altar. Neither pope nor architect lived to see the basilica anywhere near finished; Michelangelo's dome was not completed until 1590.

THE VATICAN OBELISK

The Vatican Obelisk, quarried and inscribed in Egypt around 600 B.C. and brought to Rome in A.D. 37, stood on the site of Nero's circus. In 1585, Pope Sixtus V decided to move the obelisk to in front of St. Peter's. In one of history's greatest engineering feats, architect and builder Domenico Fontana used five 51-foot-long levers (15.5m) to pry the 440-ton obelisk (400t) loose from its base. Forty winches and dozens of huge pulleys lowered the column onto its side in a wooden scaffold. The obelisk was pulled to its new location by 140 horses and nine hundred men, and the even more delicate task of lifting it up began. Fontana ordered complete silence from the enormous crowd that gathered to watch. But a sailor, alarmed by the way the ropes were stretching, shouted, "*Aigua ae corde!*" ("Water the ropes!"). This was excellent advice—the wetted ropes tightened up, and the obelisk was put in place.

Sixtus V mounted a cross containing a purported fragment of Christ's cross on the top of the obelisk. Shattering a medieval myth, workers broke the globe atop the obelisk and found no ashes, of Julius Caesar or anyone else. Eighty years later, Italian artist Gian Lorenzo Bernini made the obelisk the focal point of St. Peter's Square, and it stands there to this day.

The Vatican Obelisk, brought to Rome from Egypt two thousand years ago, stands in the center of St. Peter's Square.

Pope Paul V commissioned Carlo Maderna, the leading Roman architect of his time, to finish the nave (the space for the congregation) of the basilica around 1610. Maderna lengthened the nave and added the portico with its pediment and columns to the entrance of the church.

About forty years later, the great Italian baroque artist Gian Lorenzo Bernini completed the transition of the basilica from a classically inspired space to the lavish gold, marble, and mosaic building of today. He also added the massive baldachin, a gilded canopy atop four twisted golden pillars, which soars above the papal altar. Around the same time, he designed and constructed the colonnade that embraces St. Peter's Square. Since Bernini's time, the appearances of both the basilica and the square have not markedly changed.

ST. PETER'S SQUARE

The vast oval plaza in front of St. Peter's Basilica is known (inaccurately) in English as St. Peter's Square. St. Peter's Square was "designed to amaze,"[1] says Italian journalist Luigi Accatoli, who covers the Vatican. The massive white church building with its huge, semi-enclosed courtyard, punctuated by a towering ancient Egyptian obelisk, is the most visible and recognizable landmark of Vatican City.

A huge, elliptical colonnade, designed and built between 1656 and 1667 by Bernini, nearly encloses St. Peter's Square. In the colonnade, there are actually four rows of thirty-six columns each, but if a visitor stands on one of the two stone disks in the square that mark the focal points of the ellipse, the columns are lined up so perfectly they appear to be a single row.

Bernini's idea was to create a forum for the basilica, similar to the large public meeting places marked by columns that were a standard feature of life in ancient Rome. The square can hold at least two hundred thousand people, and such enormous throngs are common on major holy days such as Easter and Christmas and special events such as the canonization of a saint, the funeral of a pope, and the elevation of his successor.

Bernini's design also symbolized the church as a spiritual refuge from the sinful world, with the faithful gathered in the enfolding shelter of the colonnade. The plaza's size was dic-

tated not only by a desire to keep it in scale with the massive basilica, but to comfortably hold the entire population of Rome. Bernini more than succeeded in this goal, since Rome had only a little over twenty thousand residents in his time.

Bernini's reason for choosing the ellipse for the shape of St. Peter's Square is unclear. One interpretation is that he was harking back to ancient Rome—the Colosseum is oval, and the ancient Egyptian obelisk in the center of the square was a typical feature of Roman circuses. A more high-minded interpretation is that he was inspired by the discoveries of Copernicus and other astronomers that the orbits of the earth and planets around the sun are elliptical. In this view, the obelisk in the center thus symbolizes the sun, the center of the solar system; the pope, the center of the Church; and Christ, the center of the universe.

Thousands of people pack St. Peter's Square for holy days and special events.

THE *PIETÀ*

Michelangelo was young and unknown when he was commissioned to create a life-sized sculpture of the Virgin Mary holding the dead Jesus in her arms. One of the most famous statues in the world, the poignant *Pietà* called on the sculptor's skill and his genius.

It was extraordinarily challenging to depict a full-grown man cradled full length on a woman's lap. Michelangelo had to sculpt Mary as much larger than Jesus, but hid her giant size under the flowing robes that he carved into the bottom of the work. To the eye, both figures look perfectly proportioned and natural.

Shortly after the sculpture was unveiled in St. Peter's, Michelangelo overheard spectators attributing his work to another artist. Enraged, he carved his name on the sash that crosses the Virgin's breast, but he later regretted defacing the statue and never signed any of his other work.

Millions of people viewed the *Pietà* when it was displayed at the Vatican Pavilion at the 1964–1965 New York World's Fair, the only time it has left the Vatican. Damaged in St. Peter's by a hammer-wielding deranged man in 1972, the *Pietà* was restored and is now behind bulletproof glass in the basilica.

Michelangelo's Pietà *is one of many art treasures housed in the Vatican.*

THE SISTINE CHAPEL

No less awe-inspiring than the monumental basilica is the diminutive Sistine Chapel tucked alongside its north wall. Built between 1475 and 1481 by Pope Sixtus IV, the Sistine's dimensions are the same as those in the Old Testament Book of Kings for Solomon's Temple: 131 feet (40.23m) long, 43 feet (13.41m) wide, and 67 feet (20.7m) high. Virtually devoid of any architectural features such as arches, niches, or even windows (there are only twelve small round windows, called lunettes, near the top of the walls), art historians agree that the walls and ceiling of the Sistine Chapel were always meant to be decorated with frescoes. Sixtus's nephew, Pope Julius II, knew that Michelangelo was the man to paint them.

Michelangelo declined at first. He was a sculptor, he argued, not a painter. Popes tend to get what they want, though, and on May 10, 1508, Michelangelo began his on-the-job-training of learning the difficult art of fresco painting. Frescoes are paintings on fresh plaster (*fresco* is Italian for "fresh") with freshly mixed paints. Because it is difficult to make a change once the paint is applied to the plaster, a fresco has to be thought-out and designed before the actual painting begins. Then the painter must work quickly before the plaster dries.

Michelangelo's first design, which he and some assistants actually painted on part of the ceiling, was a static set of full-length portraits of the apostles. Dissatisfied, he had the whole ceiling replastered and began—all alone—his monumental rendering of the creation of the universe and the creation and fall of Adam and Eve. Between January 1509 and August 1511, Michelangelo painted more than four hundred larger-than-life-sized figures on the ceiling and upper walls of the papal chapel.

In the Sistine Chapel frescoes, Michelangelo's deep understanding of human anatomy and movement, coupled with his unsurpassed talents, revolutionized Western painting. The figures on the ceiling seem alive, on the verge of speaking and moving. Michelangelo personified the stories of Genesis—God creating the universe, separating the light from the darkness, creating Adam and Eve and then banishing them from Eden, and finally flooding the earth but saving Noah and his family—in a way that had never been seen before.

The Genesis story is told in nine frames that cover the ceiling, with images of biblical prophets and pagan seers seated on marble thrones extending down the vault. Michelangelo also created in paint some of the architectural features the chapel lacked, such as a framework of gray arches, which appear to be three-dimensional stone. He extended this framework down to the paintings on the side walls of the chapel, done earlier by other painters, to connect them visually to the ceiling.

The work of painting the ceiling was physically and mentally agonizing for Michelangelo. He did much of the work lying on his back on the scaffolding that hid his work from below or with his head bent backward for hours. Julius II, eager to see what his protégé was doing, was constantly climbing up for a look and badgering him to work faster.

Finally, on August 14, 1511, Julius II insisted on seeing the complete work. He had the scaffolding torn down and became the first person to be awestruck by the Sistine Chapel ceiling.

THE CONTROVERSIAL RESTORATION

In 1980, the Vatican made a controversial decision to clean the frescoes in the Sistine Chapel using a new solvent that had been shown not to alter or remove the original paint. The procedure took twelve years to complete on the ceiling alone; the restoration process for the entire chapel lasted twenty years. Critics charged that the solvent, applied in postage-stamp-sized patches and then carefully wiped off, was removing substances that Michelangelo had applied to achieve his famous light and shadow effects. They were aghast when the newly cleaned areas were revealed to be vivid and brilliantly colored.

Nevertheless, the cleaning revealed details that had been lost under four and a half centuries of dirt and soot. Visitors and most art experts, as well as Pope John Paul II, were delighted with the results. The effects of the cleaning are expected to last for at least one hundred years, aided by the installation of a new air-filtration system, which greatly reduces the amount of dust that gets into the chapel.

THE VATICAN MUSEUMS

The Vatican Museums house over a dozen separate major collections and many smaller ones. The museum complex,

Pope John Paul II presides at a ceremony in December 1999 to commemorate the restoration of the Sistine Chapel.

which includes the public areas of the Vatican (also known as the Apostolic) Palace, is one of the largest in the world. Its unequaled collections range far beyond paintings and sculptures to include rare books and ancient manuscripts, gemstones and jewelry, coins, armor and weapons, ancient art and artifacts, pagan and Christian religious and liturgical objects, and even vehicles and small dwellings. It is said that it would take a year's worth of visits to see just the works on display, let alone the thousands of artifacts and documents in storage.

The popes were the first monarchs to open their art collections to the public. They did this for several reasons. Art was a way of instructing the faithful in the stories of Christ and the saints. Antiquities from ancient Greece, Rome, and especially Egypt showed the Church's links to the past while emphasizing that it was destined to be more lasting than those vanished powers.

The genesis of the museums was when Pope Julius II moved several ancient Greek and Roman statues from his personal collection to the Vatican. In their present form, the Vatican Museums date back to the reigns of popes Clement XIV (1769–1774) and Pius VI (1775–1799), whose names grace the Pio-Clementine Museum. Apart from creating permanent galleries for the already large collection of paintings and sculptures that had been in the Vatican for centuries, the two popes tried to slow the flood of Roman antiquities that was being sold out of Italy to wealthy Europeans. The Vatican

The Vatican Museums house an art collection that is five centuries old.

began a deliberate effort to acquire the art being excavated all over the Mediterranean by the new science of archaeology and greatly expanded its holdings of classical antiquities.

Another large expansion followed the disaster of the Napoleonic invasion. In 1797, the French emperor Napoleon looted thousands of Vatican art and literary treasures and carted them off to Paris. After Napoleon's defeat in 1816, the Congress of Vienna not only ordered most of the stolen items returned, but directed that the Vatican receive paintings and sculptures stolen from churches in other parts of the Papal States. This added several famous works to the Vatican collection, including the Renaissance master painter Raphael's *Transfiguration* and the late seventeenth-century artist Caravaggio's *Deposition*.

New areas were set aside and constructed in the Vatican to re-create the museums. Several new museums were opened in the 1830s, including the Etruscan and Egyptian museums. Museums of African, south Asian, Japanese, and Chinese art, accumulated by missionaries, were started in the late nineteenth century. Expansion of both the collections and the buildings to house them continued until World War II (1939–1945), when the museums were closed and their collections packed away. The spaces were then used to shelter artworks from churches and museums in the war zone, as a warehouse for food supplies for the needy, and as housing for the many refugees the Vatican, as neutral sovereign territory, took in during the war.

Since the 1960s, a museum of contemporary religious art and one which displays papal vehicles ranging from carriages to cars have been added, and the museum complex has been updated to the most modern curatorial standards. In 2000, a large new entrance in the northwest corner of Vatican City was added to accommodate the millions of visitors who enter the museums each year.

THE VATICAN GARDENS

The papal gardens are somewhat less accessible to visitors than are the museums, despite the fact that the gardens take up about 40 percent of the land area of Vatican City. At various times in Vatican history, the gardens have served as a farm, providing food for the residents. They have also served as a sort of zoological gardens—Emperor Menelik of Ethiopia

Many Vatican City gardens are laid out in elaborate geometric patterns.

presented Pope Leo XIII with a pair of lions in the early 1900s, and ostriches, gazelles, and many kinds of poultry are said to have been kept there at various times.

Several areas of the gardens are quite old. A few sections of the ninth-century Leonine walls, the original rampart of the Vatican, still stand in the gardens. The Italian garden, a sixteenth-century boxwood labyrinth framed with Italian stone pine trees and cedars of Lebanon, survives, as does a baroque French garden famous for its fountains and jasmine. Several parts of the garden were deliberately laid out in geometric patterns to be viewed from the roof or dome of St. Peter's. The highest point in the Vatican, 245 feet (75m) above sea level, is in the garden; it is nearly level with the top of the dome of the basilica.

Much of the present layout of the gardens dates to the reign of Leo XIII (1878–1903), one of the self-styled "prisoner popes" who showed their disapproval of the new independent Italian state by never leaving the Vatican. The so-called prisoners of the Vatican—Pius IX, Leo XIII, Pius X, Benedict XV, and Pius XI, until 1929—could get outdoors only in the Vatican gardens, so they paid more attention to them than most of their predecessors or successors. Leo XIII had roads laid out so he could ride around the grounds in his carriage; he also had a vineyard planted and a hunting area set aside, though a Vatican gardener did the actual shooting.

Today, the Vatican Gardens still serve multiple purposes. Several acres are planted in vegetables and fruits that serve the dining tables of the pope and Vatican officials and provide some of the produce sold in the Vatican supermarket. Visitors' admission fees when the gardens are open for tours generate some revenue. The Vatican heliport is in the corner of the garden farthest from the basilica; the Swiss Guard uses it and other open spaces in the garden for training. The radio and television transmission tower is located in one of the far corners of the garden as well.

Near the center of the gardens stands the Vatican Observatory, in one of the few places in urban Rome beyond the reach of most of the city lights. It seems fitting that a place so focused on the spiritual has a spot where it turns its eyes to the heavens.

The History of Vatican City

Vatican City's history as a modern nation-state is less than a century old, dating to the Lateran Treaty of 1929, which established the present-day boundaries of the Vatican. The Vatican's story, however, dates back to the days of the Roman Empire. Vatican Hill, or *Acer Vaticanus*, was one of the seven hills on which Rome stood. The name may be Etruscan, from a tribe that inhabited the area before Rome was founded. By the middle of the first century A.D. Vatican Hill was the site of public gardens, an upper-class cemetery, and an amphitheater in which circuses, gladiatorial bouts, and chariot races were held.

FROM SHRINE TO BASILICA

Because early Christians believed that Peter, the chief apostle of Jesus, was martyred and buried on Vatican Hill, the site became a shrine. Constantine, the first Christian Roman emperor, began building a church there in 320. For its time, the first St. Peter's basilica was a very large building, nearly as long as the present church, though lower and narrower. Most of its interior and outdoor surfaces were covered with mosaics. In front of the basilica was a large, open square called an atrium, enclosed by columned porches. In the middle of the atrium was a fountain that gathered water from all the springs on Vatican Hill. The fountain was used for baptisms, but it also served the practical purpose of being a place for pilgrims to wash off the dirt of their journeys, as well as a source of drinking water.

Constantine also gave one of his houses in Rome, the Lateran Palace, to the Church for use as a residence for the pope. The Lateran Palace was the official residence of most of the

A Roman charioteer makes his way through a crowd on Vatican Hill.

popes until the end of the fourteenth century. Alongside the palace, Constantine built the first Cathedral of St. John and installed the cathedra, or bishop's chair, there. This made St. John's the official cathedral of the diocese of Rome, and the Basilica of St. John Lateran is still the seat of the Bishop of Rome, the pope.

Until the late thirteenth century some of the popes lived in a mansion adjacent to St. Peter's. Little is known about this first Vatican papal living quarters, but it was no monastic hermitage. "As the Emperors Charlemagne and Otto II stayed at the Vatican during their visits to Rome, Charlemagne in 781 and 800, and Otto in 980, the residence must have been imposing enough,"[2] says Rome historian Christopher Hibbert.

PAPAL POWER COMES INTO PLAY

During the nine years it took to complete St. Peter's, Constantine moved the political capital of the empire from Rome to Byzantium, which he renamed Constantinople (the present-day Istanbul). From there, Constantine and his successors hoped to stave off the waves of barbarians that were beginning to invade the eastern edges of the empire. By building St. Peter's and other churches in Rome, though, he established the ancient city as the spiritual capital of the Christian world.

Rather than preserving the empire, the move to the east led to the collapse of Roman rule in western Europe. During the fifth and sixth centuries, Rome was repeatedly sacked by barbarian tribes that swept over Europe. When the barbarian Visigoths invaded Italy in 410, Pope Innocent I persuaded their leader, Alaric, to spare the churches and major buildings in Rome. One of his successors, Leo I (440–461), faced

The Roman emperor Constantine donated the Lateran Palace (pictured in this nineteeth-century photo) to be used as living quarters for the pope.

down (or perhaps bought off) the fabled barbarian king Attila the Hun, saving the city from the destruction his horde had wreaked on northern Italy. Leo I was unable to stave off the Germanic tribe known as the Vandals a few years later, but still managed to keep them from burning down the entire city. The first St. Peter's was eventually plundered by the Goths and Vandals during the fifth and sixth centuries. By 700, the population of Rome had fallen to fewer than thirty thousand people (it was eight hundred thousand in 200), and much of the city was in ruins.

In the ensuing power vacuum in Europe, the Church was the only organized governing body, and the pope the only acknowledged central authority. The popes became civil rulers by default, first in Rome, and later up and down the Italian peninsula and even as far as Sicily and Sardinia.

In 800, Charlemagne was crowned Holy Roman Emperor in the first St. Peter's basilica.

The pope's role as a secular political leader grew larger in 753, when Pope Stephen II entered an alliance with the Franks (a Germanic tribe which had conquered most of present-day France) to defeat the Lombards, a tribe that controlled much of Italy. In return for the Franks's military help in getting back land then known as the Papal Estates and other territory that belonged to the Church, Stephen II officially blessed the usurper to the Franks's throne, Pepin the Short, thus recognizing him as the rightful king. The returned territory became known as the Papal States, the secular political kingdom of the popes until 1870.

In 774, Pepin's son, Charlemagne, came to Rome seeking the blessing of Pope Hadrian I. Charlemagne's ambition was to be emperor of all the lands that had been the western part of the empire and re-create Rome as its capital. He recognized that this would only be possible with the cooperation of the Church, but he left no doubt that he expected to be the supreme authority in this new empire. At Mass in St. Peter's on Christmas Day, 800, Pope Leo III crowned Charlemagne Holy Roman Emperor.

Rome's rebirth as an imperial capital was short-lived. In 846, the Muslim Arab Saracens sacked Rome, as well as St. Peter's and several other churches on Vatican Hill, which was outside the ancient walls of the city. "The shock of this attack, and the threat of a repetition in 849, induced Pope Leo IV to complete the work of enclosing the Basilica of St. Peter's and its surrounding buildings within a defensive wall," says historian Hibbert. "All the towns and convents in the Papal Estates bore a share of the cost, and the Emperor Lothar himself made a notable contribution."[3] The wall was begun in 847 and completed in 853. It included forty-six fortified towers and four gates. The area enclosed was somewhat larger than the modern Vatican City, and a few small segments of the Leonine wall still stand.

Though this can be said to be the first time the territory later known as the Vatican was defined, it was not yet known by that name. Leo IV named the newly protected basilica/fortress after himself—the *Civitas Leonina*, or Leo's city. The Romans, however, came to call it the *Borgo*, a name that remained in use until the fourteenth century.

THE AVIGNON PAPACY
Leo IV's walls could not protect his successors when the issue of papal supremacy over secular rulers came to a head in the late thirteenth century. The king of France, threatened with excommunication, had his ambassador to Rome kidnap Pope Boniface VIII (1294–1303). Then he saw to it that a French cardinal became Pope Clement V (1305–1314). By 1309, Clement V moved the entire papal court to Avignon, in southern France. From there, French popes and kings ran the Church for sixty-seven years.

By 1376, Pope Gregory XI decided that both the Church and the Papal States would be lost forever unless the pope returned to Rome. The Romans rejoiced, but when Gregory XI died the following year, they demanded a Roman, or at least Italian, pope. The conclave of cardinals found themselves barricaded inside a building under which a mob stacked firewood, threatening to burn the place down should the vote not go the way they wanted. The threat led to a farcical election—an elderly Roman cardinal was presented to the crowd as the new pontiff, while the cardinals fled to another building to elect a different Italian pope. He took the name Urban VI (1378–1389).

In the wake of attacks by Muslim Arab Saracens, in the 9th century Pope Leo IV ordered that the Vatican be surrounded by a defensive wall that included towers such as the one shown here.

The French cardinals declared Urban VI's election invalid and elevated the French archbishop of Geneva to the papacy. Then they ordered the new pope, Clement VII (1378–1394), to return to Avignon. This split the Church into two camps, one which recognized the pope in Rome, and the other, which held that the real pope was again in Avignon. This touched off a period known as the Great Schism.

ROMAN REBIRTH

While turmoil wracked the Church, Rome became even more run-down. Despite the efforts of the first two popes who ruled after the Avignon papacy and the subsequent Great Schism, Martin V (1417–1431) and Eugenius IV (1431–1447), when

THE GREAT SCHISM

In 1409, a council held in Pisa to attempt to end the Great Schism only made matters worse. The council deposed both the Roman and Avignon popes and elected a new pontiff, Alexander V. Neither of the sitting popes nor their political patrons accepted this solution, and Alexander V was murdered shortly afterward.

His killer was probably Cardinal Baldassare Cossa, a member of a distinguished Neapolitan family, who apparently was a pirate as well as a prelate. Now Cossa wanted to be pope.

Cossa was elected Pope John XXIII, thanks to the influence of the king of Naples. But before long his unscrupulous ways cost him the support of his patron. The king attacked and plundered Rome, but John XXIII escaped to Constance, where yet another Church council was meeting. John XXIII thought he could bully the council into recognizing him as supreme pontiff, but instead he was deposed and his papacy declared void. (Cossa so besmirched his papal name that no pope took the name John again until Angelo Roncalli succeeded Pope Pius XII in 1958 and became the "real" Pope John XXIII.)

It took two years to elect Cossa's successor. In 1417, the council elected a Roman bishop as Pope Martin V, and he, followed by Eugenius IV and Nicholas V, set about to restore the glories of the papacy, the Church, Rome, and the Vatican.

Nicholas V was crowned pope in 1447, Rome was little more than a crumbling country town.

Even damage caused by earthquakes that had struck Rome one hundred years before was still unrepaired. The quakes, on September 9 and 10, 1348, damaged St. Peter's severely. Even the top tier of the Colosseum, which by then had stood for over a thousand years, had come crashing down.

In the mid-fifteenth century, Rome was a ruined shadow of her former glory. The population was less than one-twentieth what it had been at the height of the empire; many cities in Italy, such as Florence, were significantly larger and far wealthier than Rome. If it had not been for the steady influx of pilgrims, Rome would have been even poorer than it was.

Nicholas V believed the faithful needed to see glorious buildings and uplifting art as strong, earthly witnesses for their faith. So he set about repairing the major cathedrals, the old Roman Senate, and the Vatican Palace, in which he took up residence. He also concluded that the old St. Peter's was not only beyond repair, but not imposing enough. He called in Florentine architect Leon Alberti to design his vision—a huge domed basilica. To jump-start the work, Nicholas V ordered twenty-five hundred wagonloads of stone brought from the ruins of the Colosseum. Pillaging the ancient monuments was a practice which many popes tried to prevent but could not resist.

Once begun, Nicholas V's successors continued his rebuilding programs with varying degrees of enthusiasm. The extraordinarily corrupt Sixtus IV (1471–1484), who spent his papacy promoting the careers of his illegitimate sons, nevertheless commissioned the Sistine Chapel and had some of its walls decorated by the best artists of his day, including Sandro Botticelli. (Michelangelo's famous frescoes were added between 1508 and 1511.) Sixtus IV also greatly enlarged the Vatican Library. Alexander VI (1492–1503), the last of the popes from the wealthy and unruly Borgia family, enlarged the Vatican Palace with the Borgia Tower and built himself a series of rooms that were decorated by the painter Pinturicchio. But it was the popes of the sixteenth century who shifted the Vatican's renaissance into high gear.

Julius Seizes the Day

Alexander VI's successor, the strong-willed, dynamic Julius II, was a man of action. When there was revolt in the Papal States, he quelled it in person, as the head of a professional papal army he raised himself. (Julius II's army became the Swiss Guard.) When he decided to tear down the original St. Peter's and build a new basilica, no amount of opposition could dissuade him. The old cathedral was demolished, and the architect Donato Bramante began the century-long job of building the largest church in the world.

Not content with a new St. Peter's, Julius II spent lavishly on the Vatican Palace and its surroundings. He hired Raphael to decorate his personal apartments, where the young painter executed some of his most striking works, including *The Disputation of the Sacrament, The School of Athens,* and *The Deliverance of St. Peter.*

This scene from the ceiling of the Sistine Chapel shows the creation of Adam.

Julius II ordered the construction of the first Roman pleasure garden since the time of the Caesars; this became the foundation of the Vatican Gardens. The pope then moved his personal masterpieces of classical sculpture, the *Apollo* and the *Laocoön,* to a courtyard that became known as the Belvedere. Possibly Julius II's most significant move, however, was to bring to Rome a brilliant but difficult young artist named Michelangelo Buonarroti.

Julius II originally hired Michelangelo to build him a magnificent tomb, but in 1508 the pope decided the sculptor was the right man to complete the decoration of the Sistine Chapel. Despite a turbulent relationship between pope and artist, Julius II celebrated Mass in the Sistine on October 31, 1511, beneath the magnificently frescoed ceiling. Four months later he was dead, but Julius II's artistic and architectural legacy is still visible in Vatican City today.

LIFT HIGH THE CROSS

Nicholas V's vision of a huge, domed basilica was finally realized in 1590, when a cross containing pieces of wood venerated as fragments of Christ's cross was raised atop the dome. About fifteen years later, the astonishingly gifted Gian Lorenzo Bernini began his first papal commission, a portrait bust. By the time he died in 1580, Bernini had left his mark everywhere on the Vatican. But while exuberant building was still the norm in the Vatican and Rome in general, the popes of this era were stern ascetics who realized that the excesses and moral lapses of their predecessors were a major factor in the Reformation and the splitting of the Christian Church into Catholicism and Protestantism.

POWERLESS POPES

The Counter-Reformation, which had begun with the Council of Trent (1545–1563), imposed strict discipline and acknowledgement of papal authority on the clergy and members of the Church. Faced with diminished political clout in nations such as Britain and Holland, which embraced Protestantism, popes sought to consolidate their positions of influence in Catholic countries such as Spain and took repressive measures against Jews and suspected heretics in the Papal States. A series of pontiffs who asserted their spiritual and temporal power in Rome and the Papal States diminished the local influence of Roman and other aristocratic families, but the popes failed to regain their former respect in the rest of Europe. When the Church was stripped of properties and power by the Revolution in France in 1789 and the Catholic king Louis XVI and his family were beheaded, Pope Pius VI virtually acknowledged his helplessness by saying he would have nothing to say. "To speak in such times of trouble and disturbance can only make bad worse,"[4] he said.

The lack of political power of the popes was further shown in 1798, when Napoleon occupied Rome and exiled the dying Pius VI to Siena. In a few weeks, the French forces looted the Vatican and the city. In 1808, Napoleon annexed Rome and the Papal States to the French Empire. Pope Pius VII (1800–1823) retaliated by excommunicating him but was driven into an exile that lasted six years.

In 1816, the Congress of Vienna undid the conquests of Napoleon and restored the power of the pope in the Papal States. Although Rome and the Papal States had suffered greatly under the French occupation, French reforms granting more individual freedoms and political participation had been welcome. The popes rolled back these reforms and, seeing modern challenges arising on all sides, sought to clamp down harder than before. One, Gregory XVI (1831–1846), imprisoned over four hundred people for their

THE PAPAL STATES

The territory known as the Papal States existed for over eleven hundred years, from 753 until 1870. The size of the pope's secular kingdom varied; in 1859 it covered more than 16,000 square miles (41,440 sq. km) of central Italy, including the present-day regions of Latium, Umbria, Marche, and Emilia-Romagna. At various times, the Papal States included Sardinia, Sicily, and Naples.

The degree of control the popes had over their territories also varied. Some popes could afford to defend their territory militarily, but by the eighteenth century, the Vatican could not afford armies. Its political influence dwindled as well. When Napoleon invaded in 1796, the pope had no allies and offered no resistance. After Napoleon's defeat, the Papal States were restored but placed under Austrian protection.

When Italian nationalism arose in the mid-nineteenth century, the pope was again powerless to resist. Several states voluntarily joined the nationalists, and in 1862, the nationalist general Garibaldi took military control and unified the entire Italian peninsula. Rome remained the pope's only temporal kingdom until 1870, when the new Italian king, Victor Emmanuel II, moved into the Quirinal, the former papal palace. Calling the new nation invalid, Pius IX retreated into the Vatican and proclaimed himself a prisoner there. This ended the Papal States and the popes' secular rule over anywhere other than Vatican City.

political beliefs and even went so far as to prohibit railroads in the Papal States, fearing they would make it easier for protestors to get to Rome.

The popes had little defense against the rising tide of nationalism in Italy. The newly created kingdom of Italy absorbed the Papal States of Romagna, Umbria, and Marche in 1860 by the vote of their own residents. Rome itself was taken by Italian forces under the command of King Victor Emmanuel II in 1870 and made the capital of the new nation. In protest against what he considered an occupation by an illegal government, Pope Pius IX abandoned the longtime papal residence in Rome, the Quirinal Palace, and withdrew behind the walls of the Vatican. There he and his successors, the self-proclaimed prisoners of the Vatican, would stay until 1929.

THE LATERAN TREATY

The resolution of the nettlesome "Roman Question" came from an unlikely source—the Fascist dictator and atheist, Benito Mussolini. He struck a deal with Pope Pius XI, which traded the Holy See's recognition of the kingdom of Italy for sovereignty and independence for Vatican City. The Lateran Treaty, signed by Mussolini as the representative of King Victor Emmanuel III and by Cardinal Gasparri for the pope, established Roman Catholicism as the official religion of Italy, which gave the Church power over things such as marriage and religious education in public schools. In return, the Church pledged that no Catholic organizations would participate in politics, a promise that gutted organized political opposition to fascism.

Mussolini apparently believed his concessions would buy at least the Vatican's silence, if not its cooperation. Instead, as early as 1931, Pius XI and later, his successor Pius XII (1939–1958), became vociferous critics of the Fascist government. (Pius XI broke with tradition by writing his anti-Nazism encyclical in German and his anti-fascism encyclical in Italian instead of the traditional Latin.) When World War II began, the officially neutral Vatican, as well as the many monasteries, convents, and churches in Rome that were recognized as extraterritorial parts of Vatican City, became refuges for dissidents, young men trying to escape military service, escaped POWs, and later, Jews. The German occupation of Rome during the war caused terror and hardship among Romans. Though the Vatican refrained from pointed criticism of the atrocities of the occupiers for fear of reprisals against the faithful, one hundred thousand people a day were fed at St. Peter's Square.

Finally, in early June 1944, with the Allied armies approaching Rome, Mussolini insisted the city had to be defended street by street. Pius XII issued a warning: "Whoever raises a hand against Rome will be guilty of matricide to the whole civilized world, and in the eternal judgment of God."[5] Apparently he struck a chord with Adolf Hitler, who ordered the German occupation forces to withdraw without a fight. The U.S. Fifth Army marched into a somewhat tattered, but undamaged, Rome.

Pope Pius XII (center, hands clasped) led the Roman Catholic faithful during the German occupation of Rome in World War II.

   Less than twenty years later, Pope John XXIII convened an even more momentous "occupation" by summoning the Catholic bishops of the world to the Second Vatican Council in 1962. During the next two and a half years, the leaders of the Church set Catholicism on a path of liturgical change, ecumenical outreach to other religions, and activism in international affairs that drastically altered nearly every aspect of Catholic life for both the clergy and the laity.

Historians and political scientists agree that losing secular political power gave the popes far more independence and influence, both in Italy and the world. With priests and bishops no longer under the power and influence of various national governments (with a few exceptions), the Church's income and property relieved of taxation (in most places), and the pontiff's status as leader of the largest religious denomination in the world, the pope is now one of the most influential forces on the world scene today.

3

THE GLORY AND THE POWER

Vatican City is one of the world's greatest spiritual centers. It is also, in the words of Jesuit scholar and editor Thomas Reese, "the headquarters of the largest multinational organization in the world."[6]

Though Vatican City is completely surrounded by Rome, life inside its walls has a unique flavor. British journalist and Vatican observer George Bull calls it "the Vatican's air of prayerful matter-of-factness"[7]—distinct from that of the bustling Italian capital. Its days are marked by ringing bells, which call the faithful to attend masses or to pause for the Angelus, the three-times-a-day prayer (6 A.M., noon, and 6 P.M.) to the Virgin Mary. Its year is measured less by the calendar or the seasons than by the liturgical seasons—Advent, Christmas, Lent, Easter, Pentecost. An average day brings thousands of visitors. Special feasts like Christmas and Easter bring tens of thousands. And milestone events—the canonization of a saint, the funeral of a pope, or the installation of a new pope—draw hundreds of thousands of pilgrims to St. Peter's Square.

Faith and fervor are unabashedly displayed publicly in Vatican City. Behind the scenes, in places the faithful seldom see, the work of running the world's largest religion gets done. Like any workplace, the Vatican has its politics. But it is a business with a mission, which, it believes, is nothing less than the spiritual salvation of its followers.

"THIS IS PETER'S HOUSE"

Many of the people who come to Vatican City are tourists, drawn by the lures of art, architecture, and antiquity. The vast majority of those who visit, though, are pilgrims. They come

A nun prays in St. Peter's Square in 2002.

to have their spirits lifted by the statues, frescoes, crosses, and the soaring dome of St. Peter's. But their chief reason is to pray, as individuals and as a community, in a place that has been venerated for two thousand years and to share the liturgies of the Roman Catholic Church. This, they believe, binds them in a special way to God and one another.

Reverend Edward Domin, a Pennsylvania priest who spent six years studying at the North American Seminary in Rome, says:

In some ways, it's probably hard for people who aren't members of the Catholic Church to understand what's really going on when they are at a ceremony in the Vatican. On the other hand, I think anyone with any sense of spirituality will recognize the depth of meaning in the liturgies. Forty percent of the people at Pope John Paul's funeral were not Catholic, but clearly they were sharing in it. But I think Catholics have the deepest experience there. They've come to see what they have learned about their faith, and to share it with one another and their Pope.[8]

*A woman prays in St.
Peter's Square during
the inaugural mass of
Pope Benedict XVI in
April 2005.*

Dozens of masses are said daily inside St. Peter's, though
always on the forty-four side altars around the basilica.
Masses on major feasts such as Christmas and Easter, which
are said by the pope, are celebrated at the papal altar beneath the baldachin. Then the pope is surrounded by cardinals, bishops, and priests who celebrate with him. Liturgies
and ceremonies which involve the pontiff are stately, tradi-
tion-steeped affairs, performed with slow reverence and

beautiful music. Usually, Catholics from all over the world are invited to play roles in such services, such as reading from the Bible or presenting to the pope the bread and wine to be consecrated.

Masses that usually draw very large crowds are held in St. Peter's Square. Father Domin was a deacon for Pope John Paul II for a Palm Sunday Mass, which was also World Youth Sunday, and cherishes a photograph of himself alongside John Paul II in the procession to the altar. "I stood up there three feet away from the Holy Father, and I said to myself 'What are you doing here?' Then I looked out at 200,000 other young Catholics, and I felt like I just belonged there."[9]

To illustrate the depth of feeling many Catholics have for the pope and Vatican City, Vatican correspondent John Allen tells the story of a late-night encounter with Cardinal Christoph Schönborn in St. Peter's Square:

"You want to know why I'm really here?" he [Schönborn] asked, in his polished English.

I [Allen] waited.

"Because Peter is here," he said.

"What?"

"Peter is here," he repeated. "He was crucified alongside this obelisk when it was in the Neronian circus, just over there," he said, pointing beyond the Palazzo di Sant'Ufficio. "But Peter is also up there, in the papal apartment, watching over the Church, just as he has been doing for two thousand years. It's an awesome sensation, standing in the space that has been the focus of a tradition that goes back to Christ himself, and to the prince of the apostles. This is Peter's House."[10]

LAST BASTION OF A "DEAD" LANGUAGE

For centuries, another tradition that connected the Vatican back to the early days of Christianity was Latin. Until the late 1960s, the Catholic Church's Mass and other religious services were conducted almost entirely in Latin; only scripture readings and the sermon were spoken in the local language. All official Vatican pronouncements were (and still are) in Latin, the language of the Roman Catholic Church since the third century.

In the 1960s, the Second Vatican Council decreed that the prayers and rubrics (directions for liturgies) that had defined Catholic practices since the Renaissance be updated and translated. This led to the gradual elimination of Latin from all Catholic ceremonies.

Latin is still the official language of Vatican City, but Church documents go out in dozens of languages, because even most of the clergy cannot read Latin adequately. Though parts of the liturgy for the funeral of Pope John Paul II in April 2005 and that of the installation of his successor, Benedict XVI, were in Latin, major portions of both ceremonies were conducted in Italian. Nevertheless, this first-century language is still used in the twenty-first century because of its adaptability.

Originally, Latin was not the language of the Church. The first Christians worshipped and read scripture in Greek, the common language of the eastern Mediterranean. When Christianity spread into the farther reaches of the Roman Empire where Latin was the common tongue, such as Africa and France, the words of the liturgy and the Bible had to be translated so people could understand. There were many regional Latin dialects, so Church leaders such as St. Augustine of Hippo (a city in present-day Libya) incorporated nonclassical (slang, in other words) Latin words into their writing and preaching to communicate with their faithful. This was the basis for ecclesiastical Latin, which allows the invention of new words for the ancient Roman tongue.

The true creator of ecclesiastical Latin was the Carthaginian priest Tertullian. While translating the Bible and early Christian writings, he had to find words for new theological concepts that had no expression in the classical forms of either Latin or Greek. Thus, he coined *baptisma* ("baptism"), *charisma* ("charisma," which means "blessing" in this sense), *ablution* ("absolution"), and even some words that we use in English today: *martyr* and *persecutor*.

After the fall of the Roman Empire, Latin evolved over several centuries into French, Spanish, Portuguese, and Italian. Only the educated members of society spoke Latin, making

THE *SCAVI* OF ST. PETER'S

The graves of rich Roman pagans lie beneath one of the most revered Christian churches in the world. The *Scavi*—Italian for "excavation"—is the now-underground "city of the dead" which topped Vatican Hill in the first century A.D. Steady archaeological digging since the site was discovered in 1940 has revealed walls, streets, and benches, as well as stone monuments and inscriptions in memory of the dead Romans interred there. The *Scavi* is so large that it takes several minutes to walk from its entrance alongside the south wall of St. Peter's to the red, graffiti-covered wall that is believed to mark the bones of Peter the Apostle.

Large as the *Scavi* is, more people get to see the pope in a month than are admitted into its tunnels in an entire year. Only a few visitors are allowed at one time, because the passageways are narrow and low and the antiquities delicate. It is necessary to book a tour months in advance to see the *Scavi*. But the effort is worth it, says Reverend Edward Domin, who studied for the priesthood in Rome, in an interview with the author, "The *Scavi* is the best thing to see in Europe, especially for Catholics, because here is Peter, with whom it all began."

it the language not only of religion, but politics, diplomacy, and science. This bolstered both Church and political rulers' control over their subjects, since every important religious and secular event in the common people's lives was carried out in a language they could not understand.

Translating the Bible into words people actually spoke became a key element of the Protestant Reformation. The Council of Trent, the Church's response to the Reformation, allowed preaching and scripture reading to be done in the local language but codified the Latin Mass and other liturgies into forms that were used until the Second Vatican Council in the 1960s. At that time, the pope and bishops agreed that the Latin Mass should be abandoned for a newer form of liturgy, which would allow the people in the pews both to understand and participate.

Though somewhat marginalized, ecclesiastical Latin survives. Its linguists still create new Latin words to express ideas and developments that could never have occurred to

This eighteenth-century coin depicts an archbishop kneeling at the feet of Jesus Christ.

Tertullian. So today we have *propaganda*— derived from the Vatican's need in the sixteenth century for a Latin word for spreading the faith. The Vatican heliport is known as *helicopterorum portus*. Ecclesiastical Latin may be all but unspoken today, but it is far from dead.

THE CENTER OF THE POWER

Likewise, Vatican City's ancient buildings bustle with modern activity. Amid the stunning architecture, the staggering collection of art masterpieces, and the sublime spiritual atmosphere of the Vatican lie—offices. Vatican City provides the work spaces for the people who conduct both the spiritual and material work of the Roman Catholic Church.

The Vatican houses three separate administrations: one for the State of Vatican City, one for the diocese of Rome, and the third, and largest, for the Holy See. It is interesting to note that the Vatican's role as the administrative center of the Roman Catholic Church dates back only to 1870. When the pope was the political monarch of Rome and the Papal States, as well as the spiritual and actual ruler of the Roman Catholic Church, the day-to-day administrative work was done in the chancellery of the Basilica of St. John Lateran (the cathedral of the diocese of Rome and the pope's seat as the bishop of Rome) or in the Quirinal Palace, which was the principal papal residence from about 1690 until it was seized by the new kingdom of Italy in 1870. From being scattered around Rome, all the offices of the Curia had to gather behind the walls of the Vatican, and there, for the most part, they remain today.

THE ROMAN CURIA

The Roman Curia helps the pope govern the Church. The word *curia* is Latin and originally meant "court," as in royal court, not court of law. The Curia is essentially the civil service of the Holy See. The 2,659 workers in the Curia—744

The Vatican City Flag

The flag of Vatican City has two vertical fields, yellow on the left and white on the right. The Holy See's coat of arms is in the center—two crossed keys, one gold and one silver, topped by the papal three-tiered crown, with two ribbons draped over the keys, whose shafts and handles are joined by a red, tasseled cord.

The three-tiered golden crown, or *triregnum*, was used by popes for ceremonial occasions for centuries, until Paul VI declined to be crowned with it in 1963. (It has not been used since.) The crossed keys refer to Christ's words to Peter: "I will give you the keys to the kingdom of heaven," and they are seen as a symbol of authority, which has been handed down from Peter through each of the popes.

The red cord symbolizes the shed blood of Jesus. The plates of the keys always contain a cross shape, but the designs of the keys' shafts and handles differ between the flag and the coat of arms of the Holy See.

The flag, which is found in most Roman Catholic churches, is flown from Vatican buildings on Catholic holy days, papal anniversaries, and special state occasions.

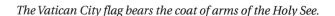

The Vatican City flag bears the coat of arms of the Holy See.

ordained men, 351 monks and nuns, and 1,564 laypeople, according to John Allen, who also notes that the majority of the laypeople occupy lower-ranking jobs—set worldwide policies for the Church, according to the pope's direction and Church law. Decisions on such issues as which prayers are used in Catholic liturgies or who can remarry in the Church following a divorce are made in the Curia. In addition, the Curia studies international issues such as Third World nations' debt and capital punishment and formulates the Holy See's positions and policies on such issues.

The power of the Curia and its secretive nature have made it controversial. There are people both inside and outside the Catholic Church who accuse the Curia of being an archaic, self-perpetuating bureaucracy, out of touch with the real world. On the other hand, "because of its relatively small size and vast jurisdiction, [others] consider it the most efficient bureaucracy in the world,"[11] says Thomas Reese. Both views have some merit, he says. The Curia has developed over the

Three cardinals converse after a meeting with Pope John Paul II in December 2002.

centuries in response to specific needs and conditions. While this means that it is largely run by entrenched insiders, Reese maintains that this has also resulted in a Curia that is not static and that has long since learned how to adapt to changing times. Allen, however, points out that true decision-making power in the Curia lies in the hands of only about five hundred people, virtually all of them ordained.

In terms of its organization, the Curia has three tribunals (the Apostolic Penitentiary, which deals with excommunications; the Roman Rota, which deals with all issues of justice in the Church, though most of its cases deal with marriage annulments; and the Apostolic Signatura, which acts as a supreme court in Church jurisdiction disputes), nine congregations (in charge of missionary activity, bishops, clergy, education, worship, beatification and canonization of saints, and doctrinal purity), and eleven councils, which oversee policy on topics such as family life, justice, health care, ecumenism, the laity, and communications.

Though each of these different dicasteries, as they are known, is headed by a cardinal and reports directly to the pope, their powers and status in the Vatican differ. The tribunals have authority over the most serious aspects of Church governance. The congregations also exert major power in the Church; for example, the Congregation for Catholic Education controls who can teach or receive honorary degrees at certain Catholic universities. They are also charged with promoting the Church's policies and views in their particular area. The councils are primarily advisory and information-gathering bodies, though some have some authority to set policy in their fields.

The membership of each congregation and council varies, and not all members are residents in the Vatican or even in Rome. Though the members are nearly all clergy, there are some laypeople. For example, on the Council for the Laity, Council for the Family, and Council for Justice and Peace, says Reese, the lay members outnumber the ordained. The councils and congregations meet on their own schedules, some several times a year, others at longer intervals.

Between meetings, their work is supported and carried out by professional staffs, which vary in size. "None are very large by secular government standards," says Reese. "Only three dicasteries had more than 30 professionals, including

The Pope's American Organist

Perhaps the most visible American in the Vatican is organist Peter Goettsche. Since 1989, he has held the dual jobs of official organist for both the pope and St. Peter's, which means he provides music for most of the services in the basilica.

Born in Los Angeles in 1942, Goettsche taught himself to play the organ as a child. He also taught himself Italian and dreamed of playing in Italy. He realized his dream in 1961, when he met Fernando Germani, one of Europe's best organists. Germani invited Goettsche to attend his school in Rome, from which Goettsche graduated in 1968.

Goettsche works with the committee that decides on the music for liturgies that the pope celebrates. "Apart from that, I have almost complete liberty over what music is performed in St. Peter's," he says in an interview with the author. He has even introduced the music of Bach into the Vatican, even though the German composer is closely identified with the Protestant Reformation. "I feel like I'm living a part of history," says Goettsche. "My life has exceeded my wildest dreams."

typists and technicians, in 1994 . . . some dicasteries have fewer than 10 professionals."[12]

One major and fairly speedy change in the Curia has occurred since the 1970s—the internationalization of its members. Before Paul VI (1963–1978) began appointing priests and laypeople from around the world, the Curia was almost totally staffed and run by Italians. In 1961, ten of the eleven congregations were headed by Italian cardinals, and over 80 percent of all the professional staff was Italian as well. Paul VI's efforts at internationalization were aided by the swift decline in Latin as the universal language of the Church, which made it necessary to have speakers of many languages running things in the Vatican. Thus, by 1994, roughly half of the Curia's professional staff was not Italian.

Nevertheless, Italian is still the working language of the Curia (Pope Benedict XVI's first public pronouncements were in Italian, and he conducted much of John Paul II's funeral in that language), and most of the Curia members with the longest careers are Italian. Most people inside the Curia agree, however, that the current cosmopolitan makeup is a good thing, bringing in people with differing experiences and perspectives, as well as deeper insights into the life of the Church in Asia, Latin America, and Africa.

Despite the new internationalism in the Curia, the number of women working in Curia posts is still quite low. About 10 percent of the four hundred staffers in the most important dicasteries are women, the Catholic News Service reported in 2004. There are some nuns with professional training, such as canon lawyers, as well as professional laywomen, who work mostly in the dicasteries concerned with finances, family and social issues, and ecumenism. In some of those councils, women make up one-third of the staff.

The physical offices of the Curia are clustered mostly in the Apostolic Palace (also known as the Vatican Palace), the four-story building whose front facing St. Peter's Square contains the private apartment of the pope. The Curia shares this one-thousand-room building not only with the pontiff, but with the Vatican Bank, the Secret Archives, and the Sistine Chapel. Despite these opulent surroundings, Curia offices tend to be sparsely furnished and low-tech, writes John Allen, who has seen the inside of many of them. The offices of the government of Vatican City, on the other hand, have their own large, four-story building directly behind St. Peter's.

The Curial workday runs from 8:30 A.M. to 1:30 P.M., Monday through Saturday. Twice a week, usually Tuesdays and Fridays, staff members return to their offices from 4:00 P.M. to 7:00 P.M. This schedule seems curious to Americans, but it matches up with the hours many people work in the city of Rome. It also accommodates the second careers of many Curia workers; many of the clergy have church or teaching duties in addition to their Vatican jobs, and many of the laypeople work second jobs to augment their salaries, which can be low (though tax free and very secure) relative to similar jobs in Rome.

A thirty-six-hour workweek should not be taken as a sign that Curialists do not work hard, says John Allen. For the most part, they tend to give their lives over to their jobs, believing, as they do, that they are serving the Church and the world in a divine cause.

4

THE WORLD'S SMALLEST SUPERPOWER

John Paul II restored the Roman Catholic Church to a position of prominence and influence in world affairs that it had not enjoyed for centuries. His charismatic personality and tireless travels around the world raised the Church's profile on the international stage. Beyond embodying the Roman Catholic Church to the world, John Paul forced a dramatic shift in Vatican foreign policy—from compromise with the Church's challengers to direct, though never political, confrontation. Convinced of the truth of his Church's teachings, the pope called attention to many governments that prevent their people from living and acting according to their own beliefs.

POWER OF A POLISH POPE

Historians and political scientists differ on what papal actions and words—if any—contributed directly to the anti-Communist revolution in Poland and the rest of Eastern Europe. It is clear, however, that the presence of their dynamic fellow countryman at the head of their beloved Catholic Church galvanized the Poles into action in the early 1980s. In addition, it is known that the Vatican and the U.S. government were in close communication during the years leading up to the collapse of European communism, though neither nation played an immediate, active role in the overthrow of the Soviet-puppet governments of Eastern Europe.

John Paul II's relentless insistence on basic human rights for all brought him both admiration and criticism—sometimes from the same quarters. For example, the U.S. State Department is believed to have worked closely with diplo-

Pope John Paul II walks past the crowd during a visit to Chicago in 1979.

mats from the Holy See as well as the pope himself during the end of the Cold War. When John Paul included a personal audience for Fidel Castro during his visit to Cuba in 1998, however, the United States was less than enthusiastic.

It should not be forgotten, however, that several of John Paul II's predecessors in the twentieth century also took actions in international affairs. Nor should the steady, often subtle impact of the Holy See in the dozens of international bodies to which it belongs or sends delegates or observers be overlooked. No other religious body in the world acts as a sovereign state in international politics, though this state's only weapons are persuasion and moral authority—and 1.1 billion followers.

THE POLISH POPE

Pope John Paul II shattered modern papal stereotypes. Elected on October 16, 1978, at the age of fifty-eight, he was the youngest pope in over 130 years, the first non-Italian pope since 1523, and the first pope to visit a Communist nation. Athletic, outgoing, and brilliant, he brought a wide array of talents and experiences to the papacy.

Born in 1920 in Wadowice, Karol Wojtyla (yoy-TIH-wah) was an actor, poet, playwright, and soccer player before entering an underground seminary to study for the priesthood while Poland was still under Nazi rule in 1942. Ordained in 1946, he taught at Poland's Catholic university, becoming an internationally respected scholar. He became visible by dealing with Poland's repressive Communist government as archbishop of Kraków, and at the young age of forty-seven he was elevated to Cardinal.

Nevertheless, the Church, the world, and Wojtyla himself were stunned by his election to the papacy. John Paul II quickly shattered papal precedents as he skied, swam, visited 118 countries, traveled over 600,000 miles (966,000km), and became the most visible pope in history. Strongly orthodox and conservative in his views of Church teaching, John Paul

spoke forcefully on issues such as human rights and is considered among the most influential people of the twentieth-century. He died on April 2, 2005, his twenty-six-year reign the third longest of any pope.

Polish cardinal Karol Wojtyla became Pope John Paul II in 1978.

THE DIPLOMATIC SERVICE

Why does a religious body need a foreign policy and a diplomatic corps? One answer lies in the history of the Church and in the pope's former role as a secular ruler. In many ways, the Holy See can be said to have invented diplomacy. Popes have been sending out ambassadors longer than any other rulers on earth. As individual kingdoms arose in Europe in the Middle Ages, the Church needed the means both to communicate with the bishops, priests, and faithful in a given region and to exert its political influence on the ruler.

Another consideration was defense. Even when the Papal States were at their largest geographic size, most popes did not have the financial resources to raise armies; if they needed military might for some reason, they had to have allies with armies. So popes began sending personal representatives to their fellow sovereigns. These representatives soon learned that, even though they were backed by the pope's moral authority and his power to excommunicate uncooperative monarchs, they needed both negotiation skills and the ability to compromise and build consensus with kings and emperors.

The five hundred or so people who represent the Holy See abroad are the pope's diplomatic arm, as well as his eyes and ears around the world. These ecclesiastical gypsies spend most of their careers in one or another of the 214 papal nunciatures, as the Holy See's embassies are called (the papal ambassador is called a nuncio). There are nunciatures in nearly every nation on earth except China, North Korea, Vietnam, and Saudi Arabia.

Papal diplomats carry out many roles. They deal with the Catholic cardinals and bishops of the nation where they are stationed, as well as with the national government. Another of their most important functions is to promote the Church's foreign policy objectives, chief of which are peace, human rights, justice, and environmental protection. Another key role, particularly in totalitarian nations, is to protect the Church's financial assets and/or property, as well as the safety and freedom to worship of Catholics and other believers. A third role that Vatican diplomats have played, or at least attempted to play, is that of peacemakers or neutral mediators in international disputes, such as between Israel and Palestine over the holy places in Jerusalem.

ALL THE POPE'S MEN

The Holy See's diplomats are all priests, trained at the Pontifical Ecclesiastical Academy in Rome. The diplomatic corps was almost entirely Italian until the 1970s; now they are drawn from all over the world. At any given time, there are about thirty-two priests studying in the academy, which American journalist John Allen describes as "the West Point of the Vatican civil service."[13] The course of study lasts four years. When they have completed it, academy graduates have at least a degree, if not a doctorate, in canon law or theology, as well as a solid grounding in languages, international law, and Church and diplomatic history. Daily life at the academy is set up to instruct the students in high-level etiquette, from the intricacies of protocol to which fork to use. Students have also been led through a process of personal and spiritual formation, which aims to ensure that Vatican diplomats are both world-wise and committed to the Church, good people as well as good priests, sensible, level-headed, and capable of creating a dialogue with anyone.

Academy graduates are sent to be assistants to nuncios, which is a form of on-the-job training. They can expect to spend about three years in any given post and to spend eighteen to twenty years as an assistant. There are five ranks in the diplomatic service: *addetto*, or attaché; secretary; *uditore*, or listener; counselor; and nuncio. Diplomats can also expect to work at intervals in the Vatican itself, in the offices of the Secretariat of State. It is there that they can best attract the attention of high-level Church officials.

In many ways, the members of the Vatican diplomatic corps are the consummate Curia insiders, as well as its elite. Because they have direct knowledge of local churches and cultures, they are better able to interpret the information that comes into the Curia from around the world. They have numerous contacts and friends in many countries. They can speak, read, and write in several languages. All these information and communication assets are key to advancing a career in the Curia.

Access to information is the greatest strength of the Holy See's diplomatic efforts. Even though it has fewer than seven hundred people in the field or working inside the Vatican (the support staff in the Vatican offices numbers less than two hundred), the Holy See's unique position in the world al-

Priests attend a class at the Regina Apostolorum Pontifical Academy, a Vatican-affiliated university founded in 1993 for the study of philosophy, theology, and bioethics.

lows it access to unequaled sources of information. As John Allen puts it in *All the Pope's Men*:

> The nuncio in every country on earth has access to a network of intelligence and perspective that any spy agency would envy: the local church, meaning the local clergy and bishops, who know the situation, the people,

and the language from the inside out. When the Vatican wanted to understand the impact of the UN sanctions on Iraq during the 1990s, for example, it did not have to send observers or commission studies. It could simply phone the head of the 1-million-strong Chaldean Catholic Church in Baghdad, or the archbishop of the Latin rite, and ask for impressions. The nuncio and Secretariat of State also have access to the vast network of missionary communities in the Catholic Church, who have missionary priests, brothers, and sisters in every nook and cranny of the planet. Nuncios who know how to deploy these assets can be among the best-informed members of any diplomatic corps.[14]

Cardinals and archbishops from around the world, members of the Vatican's diplomatic corps, meet in France in 2005.

✠ A MEMBER OF THE CLUB

Today, the Holy See has full diplomatic relations with 174 nations, up from 92 at the beginning of John Paul II's reign in 1978. It also holds either membership or observer status in forty-three regional and international intergovernmental organizations. These bodies include the World Health Organization; the International Atomic Energy Agency; the UN Conference on Trade and Development; the International Telecommunications Union; the World Food Program; the UN Educational, Scientific and Cultural Organization; and even the World Tourist Organization. The Vatican is a signatory to the Nuclear Non-Proliferation Treaty and a delegate to the Arab League. Participation in such groups allows the Church to make its views on human rights heard in major policy-making circles.

Another key to the Holy See's influence in certain world affairs is its neutrality. The Vatican tends to be open and transparent about its foreign policy aims (as opposed to its operations), which gives it the freedom to comment and work as a neutral party in certain international disputes without being suspected of having a private agenda or hidden interests. Since it is not part of any power bloc or economic system, its working relationships are not confined to its own "side." Because it maintains official contacts, as well as Church lines of communication, with virtually every country on earth, the Holy See often knows more about a situation than any of the parties involved. It can approach all sides embroiled in a controversy and assure them of its objectivity, as well as its legendary discretion and ability to keep secrets.

PULLING OPEN THE IRON CURTAIN

It was the Vatican's broad and deep well of information which the United States apparently hoped to tap when the Solidarity movement in Poland began to fracture the Communist bloc. According to several published accounts, such as *His Holiness: John Paul II and the Hidden History of Our Time* by Carl Bernstein and Marco Politi, senior U.S. intelligence officials William Casey and Vernon Walters met with John Paul

II, showed him satellite photos of Soviet and Warsaw Pact troops and equipment gathering near the Polish borders, and briefed him on secret Reagan administration policies regarding the Soviet Union. In turn, the Polish pope shared his assessment of the character of the major figures on both sides—the Solidarity labor movement and the Communist government—in Poland. This kind of information was useful to the United States, particularly after its most valuable Polish spy was forced to flee the country.

The Soviet Union also courted the pope's influence in his native country, at one point promising not to take military action against the Solidarity movement if its leaders could be held in check by the Church. This was not a huge concession for the Vatican, as the pontiff had called repeatedly for restraint and only peaceful protests on the part of the labor union, all the while stressing the Church's stand that workers' right to organize is a fundamental human right. The Soviets' request was a tacit admission that the Church, and John Paul personally, had more authority in Poland than either the government or the Communist Party.

THE POPE'S REAL POWER

Several accounts of John Paul's role in the collapse of communism have been published, drawn largely from interviews with Western diplomats and policy makers who dealt with the pope and from records which became available after elected governments took over in countries such as Poland, the former East Germany, and Russia. There is little reason to doubt the reliability of these accounts, but corroboration of the Holy See's side of the story must wait until its records are made public, a notoriously slow process.

Some Catholic analysts say that interpreting the pope's pivotal role in those events solely through a political and diplomatic perspective fails to show his real power. By delivering a steadfastly spiritual message, John Paul II was able to call up the long-suppressed true history and culture of the Polish people, says George Weigel, a senior fellow of the Ethics and Public Policy Center in Washington, DC. In the prestigious Templeton Lecture on Religion and World Affairs, which he presented in 2000, Weigel maintains that John Paul believed that "overwhelming material force can be resisted successfully through the resources of the human spirit—

through culture—and that culture is the most dynamic, enduring factor in human affairs, at least over the long haul."[15] A people's culture, in this view, is indissolubly linked to its spiritual life.

John Paul II told the millions of Poles who came out to see him during the nine days of his first visit back to his homeland in 1979, "You are not who they say you are. Let me remind you who you are."[16] By calling on Poles to draw on their true cultures—which included a thousand years as a Catholic nation until being taken over by the Communists in 1946—Weigel says John Paul II set in motion a culturally-driven change that communism could not counter.

Weigel concedes that the Holy See's ability to support pro-democracy movements with discreet financial help and to

Pope John Paul II walks through the UN General Assembly in 1979. As spiritual leader of the world's 1 billion Catholics, the pope has a significant voice in world affairs.

collect information and facilitate communication between such movements played a role in the decade which finally led to the collapse of the Communist governments all over Eastern Europe. However, he argues that it was first necessary for the people of that region to assert their own national identities, of which their religion was a major feature. Despite the fact that not all the religions were Catholic—or even Christian—people responded to the pope's call to reassert their own cultures, and that led to momentous change.

MEDIATING THE BEAGLE CHANNEL DISPUTE

Another international episode that signaled the Vatican's return to international affairs was the Beagle Channel dispute. The Holy See's mediation of this long-simmering border dispute between Argentina and Chile ably demonstrated the skill of the Holy See's diplomats. They not only averted an almost certain war, but they devoted several years to bringing about a peaceful resolution.

Chile and Argentina had quarreled over a large stretch of ocean and three small islands near the southern tip of the South American continent for over a century. The dispute had wide implications of access to fishing areas and control of the strategically important Straits of Magellan. At the time, it was also believed that there were significant petroleum deposits under the seabed. War seemed inevitable by December 1978.

On December 23 that year, Pope John Paul II informed both governments that he was sending a personal envoy to both capitals on a mission of good offices. The papal mediator proved to be the first and only intermediary acceptable to both sides, predominantly Roman Catholic countries that were each ruled by military dictators. Coupled with the Holy See's moral authority, the Vatican was also clearly neutral and uninvolved in any aspect of the dispute.

The Vatican mediator, Cardinal Antonio Samoré, acted first to defuse the military crisis. Then he set up a framework for transmitting information between each of the governments. It took six years of painstaking, and sometimes creative, diplomacy on Samoré's part finally to resolve the dispute. The Vatican proposed a series of compromises over fishing rights and boundaries that both countries accepted in 1984.

Scholars of diplomacy who have studied the Beagle Channel mediation agree that it was Samoré's and the Vatican's "unique institutional patience" which ultimately led to resolution. Lawyer Mark Laudy, in his examination of the affair, writes:

> The mediation served as a kind of holding mechanism that maintained the status quo until the political developments necessary for a permanent accord had been achieved. The Pope, having a long-term perspective on his mission, and being largely unaccountable to any interested constituencies, was almost certainly better suited to such a role than other heads of state. Other governmental mediators, subject to electoral or other political pressures, might be expected to push more aggressively for a quick solution, in the interest of short-term political expediency. In a delicate political environment, such an approach might well have jeopardized the mediation process and returned the parties to the brink of war.[17]

"CIVILIZING" CHILE

One of the political developments that helped lead to a successful resolution of the Beagle Channel dispute was the overthrow of the military government in Argentina in 1983 and the restoration of a more-or-less democratic system. Argentina's new, elected rulers were far more amenable to compromise over the Beagle Channel issue than the military junta had been.

But Augusto Pinochet Ugarte's brutal dictatorship was still in place in Chile when John Paul visited there in 1987, and many Catholics were uncomfortable with what they saw as the Vatican's tacit acceptance of the regime. But the pope had also supported the Vicariate of Solidarity, founded by the archbishop of Santiago to assist victims of the regime and to press for human rights.

John Paul II realized that Chile's fractured society had to be healed before any progress to democracy could be made. Chileans were deeply divided over politics and suspicious of each other. During his visit, the pontiff exhorted the Chilean bishops to start to re-create a civil society, emphasizing the

Pope John Paul II walks with Augusto Pinochet during a 1987 visit to Chile. The pope's visit helped inspire Chileans to throw off military rule and restore democracy.

people's common bonds, such as their religion, as a means to overcome the divisions that had arisen between the pro- and anti-Pinochet factions. According to Weigel, John Paul II succeeded. In the Templeton Lecture, Weigel maintains that the pope's visit "accelerated the process of reconstructing Chilean civil society [a year and a half later], a national plebiscite (referendum) voted to move beyond military rule and restore democracy."[18]

JOHN PAUL'S LEGACY

Obviously, not every nation John Paul visited rose up shortly thereafter and threw off its political shackles the way Poland and Chile did. Though he appealed to the Cuban people to call up their unique cultural and Christian heritage and reprimanded Castro for human rights violations when he visited Cuba in 1998, the Caribbean nation remains one of the last remaining Communist regimes. Russia resisted all papal attempts to visit, though the Kremlin did allow low-level diplomatic exchanges. Vietnam, which once had a large Catholic population, and the Peoples' Republic of China are among the nations that have resisted Vatican overtures for better relations.

Possibly these nations feared John Paul II's relentless focus on human rights, particularly the right to worship for all believers, not merely Catholics. During his reign, the Catholic Church emerged as one of the most vocal critics of human rights abuses, which, in its view, include capital punishment and abortion. Observers of the Vatican expect that working for peace and human rights will continue as the heart of the Holy See's diplomacy in the twenty-first century.

5

Everyday Life in Vatican City

When Pope John XXIII was asked how many people worked in the Vatican, he is said to have replied with the Italian joke "About half of them." In fact, the two thousand or so laypeople (as well as some clergy) who fill the secular jobs in Vatican City are both proud of their work and protective of their often-inherited positions. That is because they believe their work serves a higher purpose.

The everyday functions of the Vatican are largely driven by two aims—to communicate the Church's message with the world, especially to the Catholic faithful, and to provide the services—both spiritual and mundane—that the Vatican's residents require and that its millions of visitors seek. Some jobs in the Vatican have hardly changed for centuries, while others have existed for only a few years.

But whether they carry out a simple, old job, like setting up chairs and kneelers for liturgies, or a complex, modern one such as creating and maintaining the Vatican Web sites, Vatican employees believe their work is dedicated to the pope and, through him, to God.

Spreading the Word

For centuries, popes communicated with their flock in two ways: edicts and art. Awe-inspiring churches, statues, stained glass windows, mosaics, frescoes, tapestries, and paintings told the stories of Christ and the saints to a mostly illiterate faithful. When inspiration alone did not convey the message, popes resorted to official documents (in Latin only), sent to the bishops who then transmitted the Vatican's teaching to the people.

Now, the pope must reach the world with his message. The world may be hard to reach, and the people may have trou-

Workers in April 2005 prepare the Sistine Chapel, where the cardinals of the Catholic Church traditionally meet to elect a new pope.

ble understanding the message, but this cannot deter the pope, according to British journalist George Bull, who has covered the Vatican since the 1960s. Bull continues by saying, "The essence of the purpose of the Catholic Church, and of the Papacy, armed with the Gospel—the Good News—is to communicate."[19]

John Paul II used every modern communications tool available—television, radio, Internet, and jet travel—to bring

VATICAN MOSAICS

If Vatican City can be said to have a factory, it would be the mosaic studio. Located in a building just northwest of St. Peter's, the studio is charged first and foremost with the maintenance and restoration of the mosaics that cover most of the interior of the basilica.

Shortly after St. Peter's was completed, it was realized that glass and stone were more durable than oil and canvas and more luminous than fresco, so most of the paintings in the basilica were copied into mosaics, and the originals were removed to the Vatican Museums. The mosaic studio was formally instituted by Benedict VIII in 1727.

The artisans of the mosaic studio manufacture their own medium—the opaque enamel stone tesserae and a type of glass mosaic that the Vatican bought the patent for in 1731. They can produce over thirty-two thousand hues, the largest supply of mosaic material in the world. Beyond their restoration duties, the studio's artists make copies of famous works for sale to the public and create mosaics on commission for churches and buildings all over the world. The pope frequently presents mosaics to visiting dignitaries and to the heads of the nations that he visits.

This mosaic of an angel appears in the dome of St. Peter's Basilica.

Catholic teaching directly to his followers and nonbelievers alike. He was the first pope to use e-mail; he received tens of thousands of messages during the final weeks of his life. Even before he was formally installed as pope, Benedict XVI had an e-mail address. Now, when the Vatican speaks, the faithful can talk back.

THE VATICAN PRESS

Though the Church has often been viewed as obsessed with secrecy and hostile to new ideas and technologies, the Vatican Press has operated since shortly after the printing press was invented. The Polyglot Press, as it is informally known in English, publishes and prints an enormous quantity of religious education materials in dozens of languages (hence the name "Polyglot"), official news and documents of the Curia and Holy See, annual reports and directories of Vatican and Church personnel, and the famous daily newspaper of the Vatican, *L'Osservatore Romano.*

The newspaper has been published daily in Italian since 1861 and weekly in French, English, Spanish, Portuguese, and German since the 1960s and 1970s. The newspaper prints the texts of the pope's speeches, lists his daily schedule, and publishes the names of all the officials and bishops he appoints. More importantly, the paper comments frequently in its editorials on religious, political, social, economic, and international matters. Though unsigned, the editorials are regarded as high-level policy statements and accurate barometers of where the Church stands on an issue.

VATICAN RADIO

Pope Pius XI invited the inventor of radio, Guglielmo Marconi, to bring the technology of mass communications into the Vatican in 1931. Marconi's tower still stands in the Vatican Gardens, on the highest ground in Vatican City, but now the job of transmitting Vatican Radio's round-the-clock broadcasts is handled by the world's largest rotating antenna, which is located in the countryside north of Rome.

Radio is not only a means for the Church to communicate with people around the world, although official announcements, news, papal speeches, and blessings are staples of its programming. Vatican Radio has always put a special emphasis on reaching areas of the world where there is little or

In this 1940s photo, a papal employee adjusts the equipment at the Vatican Radio station, which broadcasts programming in 40 languages to 5 continents.

no religious freedom, such as China. It has sometimes sent messages in code to bishops in areas where official communications were difficult or forbidden, and it has had occasion to act as a medium through which beleaguered, imprisoned, or exiled bishops could communicate with their own local flock. Broadcasting in thirty-five languages, Vatican Radio has been, like the BBC and the Voice of America, a source of accurate news for millions of people whose governments control what they see, read, or hear. The radio station also has its own Web site and broadcasts online.

The radio station has one of the biggest and most international staffs in the Vatican, with over two hundred people from more than three dozen countries. The senior managers of the radio are priests, but most of the workers are laypeople, and a high percentage (for the Vatican) is female.

VATICAN TELEVISION

Though the Vatican embraced the power of radio early on, television was a relative latecomer. "This has been the first pontificate in which television has been the dominant medium,"[20] said the head of Vatican television, Jesuit priest Federico Lombardi, a few weeks before the death of John Paul II. The charismatic former actor had no qualms about using television to further his mission, and he committed large sums to the establishment of the Vatican Television Center in 1983. The station went on the air in 1983 with a videotape of John Paul II's visit to Lourdes and quickly grew to hundreds of live broadcasts a year, as well as video coverage of papal journeys, meetings of church officials, and general coverage of church and Vatican news. The director of the Centro Televisivo Vaticano (CTV), as it is known, is a priest, but most of its two dozen or so employees are laypeople.

Another service of the CTV is its temperature- and humidity-controlled archive of videotapes made since 1984. One of the busiest video archives in the world, it contains over four thousand hours of recordings, though the vast majority of them date only to the 1980s.

THE VATICAN WEB SITE

A more recent technological innovation is the Vatican Web site. It was the brainchild of Joaquin Navarro-Valls, the Spanish layman who was John Paul II's press secretary, and established by an American Franciscan nun, Sister Judith Loeblein.

The Web site debuted at Christmas of 1995 with the text of the pope's traditional *Urbi et Orbi (The City and the World)* address. This opened an unprecedented interaction between the Vatican and Catholics around the world. Within two weeks, over 2.4 million people had visited the site. "Four thousand, six hundred and seventy-eight messages, in ten languages, arrived at our address in a single week!"[21] says Navarro-Valls.

On the Web site, visitors can read some of the recent documents issued by the Holy See, learn about the saints who

Vatican spokesman Joaquin Navarro-Valls comments on the failing health of Pope John Paul II in April 2005.

have been canonized during the papacy of John Paul II, read about religious ceremonies held in St. Peter's, follow the pope's schedule, or listen to the Sistine Chapel Choir. Officially, the Web site publishes in six languages (German, English, Italian, Spanish, French, and Portuguese), but not every page on the site is available in each language.

TENDING THE NEEDS

The pope may be elected, but many of the two thousand or so people who come to work in the Vatican every day have inherited their jobs. Generations of Romans have served the Vatican in all sorts of hands-on jobs—gardening, carpentering, cooking, or cleaning—that have been handed down from father to son (mostly) for generations. Though not citizens of Vatican City, they are proud and protective of their roles in its life.

According to Jesuit scholar Thomas Reese:

> Most Americans and Germans think Vatican City is inefficiently run, but in comparison with Italian bureaucracies it operates fairly well, and its profits help finance the Roman curia. The Vatican museums are better maintained and have more visitors than most Italian museums.... Likewise, the Vatican post office is very efficient . . . residents of Rome trust its services more than the Italian mail when sending a letter out of Italy.[22]

Given that only a few thousand people tend to hundreds of priceless works of art, millions of documents, huge historic buildings, forty-plus acres of gardens, 4 million visitors a year, one of the world's most visible celebrities, and the spiritual (and sometimes material) needs of 1.1 billion Catholics, Reese's assessment seems fair.

THE SWISS GUARD

Like many things in the Vatican, describing the Swiss Guard calls for superlatives. It is the smallest army in the world. It is the world's most photographed armed force. It is also far and away the oldest, with five hundred years of uninterrupted service since its founding in 1506.

The Swiss Guard began as a private mercenary army raised and personally led by Pope Julius II to quell a rebellion in a northern papal state. Only twenty-three years later, the Swiss Guard proved their valor when they stood fast to defend the besieged Clement VII (1523–1534) at the Castel Sant'Angelo against vastly superior German forces and died to the last man. The annual swearing-in ceremony of new guards is held on May 6 in remembrance of their heroism.

Today, a man must be Swiss, Catholic, reputable, physically healthy, at least 5'9" (175cm) tall, aged nineteen to thirty, and single to be eligible to join the one-hundred man company. Guards are allowed to marry, but not until they are at least twenty-five and have attained the rank of corporal. There are apartments in the Vatican for married guards, and their spouses and children also hold Vatican citizenship as long as the man is a member of the guard.

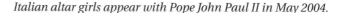 CHILDREN IN THE VATICAN

Kids make up a tiny fraction of Vatican City's population. Some are the children of lay workers whose jobs come with a residence in the Vatican, while others' fathers are Swiss Guards, who also live inside the walls. For these people, Vatican citizenship lasts only as long as they hold their positions, and their spouses and children are citizens, too.

Approximately forty-five boys between the ages of eleven and fifteen attend a Vatican boarding school for altar boys. With an average of sixty masses a day celebrated in St. Peter's alone, they are kept busy with their liturgical duties, but they do all the things boys their age do as well—trade soccer cards, play pinball, and spend time with their friends. After they reach the age of sixteen, some Vatican altar boys go on to seminaries to study for the priesthood, but most return to their homes and regular schools.

John Paul II reestablished a school in the Vatican for the boys who sing in the Sistine Chapel Choir. Though the choirboys do not live in the Vatican, their duties require them to be there a great deal of the time; an on-site school lets them combine regular subjects with music instruction, rehearsals, and singing for ceremonies.

Italian altar girls appear with Pope John Paul II in May 2004.

With their elaborate striped uniforms, halberds (lances), pointed steel helmets, and the fact that their chief duties involve liturgical and state ceremonies and standing guard at doors and gates, the Swiss Guards may have a comic opera air about them. In fact, the papal army is an integral part of the security force protecting both the Vatican and the pope himself. Members of the guard are highly trained in unarmed combat, and they also know how to use their ceremonial swords and halberds as weapons. Switzerland requires all its male citizens to take annual weapons training, so each man is certified to used handguns and automatic weapons, though the Swiss Guards do not carry firearms on duty. Since the attempted assassination of John Paul II in 1981, the guard has taken on more security duties, such as crowd control.

THE VATICAN CITY SECURITY FORCE AND CRIME

Vatican City also has a conventional police force, a necessity given its huge volume of visitors, the incalculable value of its treasures, and the ever-present threat of violence against the pope. Because of the sensitive nature of most of its duties, there is little public knowledge about the operations of the security force, but its members are most visible as security guards when the pope is out in public. Still known informally as the gendarmes, the 120-member force is credited with the quick response that saved John Paul II's life after the assassination attempt in 1981.

Even the hallowed environment of the Vatican is not crime free. The most common crimes are pickpocketing, especially when large crowds are gathered in St. Peter's Square, and shoplifting in the stores or Vatican Museums. There have been thefts, some still unsolved, from the Vatican Museums. In several cases, the perpetrator was found to be a member of the staff, but the Vatican is tight-lipped about all such incidents and their outcomes. The two most violent incidents in Vatican City since the assassination of the papal prime minister in 1848 were the attempted assassination of John Paul II in 1981 and the 1998 murder of the commander of the Swiss Guard and his wife by a junior member of the guard, who then committed suicide.

Vatican City has its own penal system and even a jail with two cells. Anyone who is sentenced to prison under the Vatican civil court is incarcerated in an Italian prison, however.

This photograph shows the attempted assassination of Pope John Paul II in St. Peter's Square in May 1981.

Vatican City's chief prosecutor reported that there were 608 crimes in 2002, the latest year for which statistics are available. Nearly all were petty theft. Considering that 3 to 4 million people visit there in an average year, those numbers suggest that the Vatican is generally a safe and tranquil enclave.

THE VATICAN FIRE DEPARTMENT

Fire is an even rarer event than crime in the Vatican. There has not been a major fire in Vatican City in more than two hundred years. The Vatican fire department has fifteen members, with three fire trucks and a hook and ladder truck, but the department can call on assistance from the firefighters of Rome if necessary. The department's daily job is to inspect St. Peter's painstakingly after closing. Two firemen assist the maintenance workers, climbing ladders to check niches and other places a person might hide or conceal a bomb.

CITY SERVICES

The government of Vatican City operates out of its own office building adjacent to the papal gardens. The city manager of Vatican City is officially known as the counselor general; until March 2005, the post was held for many years by Giulio Sacchetti, an Italian from an ancient and noble family whose members have held many posts in the Vatican. The counselor general oversees the workings of the postal service, security force (though not the Swiss Guard), fire department, pharmacy, supermarket, and nonliturgical buildings, as well as the upkeep of the streets and gardens. Part of the financial support for these city operations comes from admission fees to the Vatican Museums, which the counselor general also oversees. In most years, tourism gives the Vatican City administration a healthy profit.

The Vatican supermarket is known as the *annona*, or provision office. Access to it is strictly controlled, because prices are lower than in nearby Roman stores since they are not subject to Italian or European Union sales taxes. Another part of the *annona* sells items such as clothing, tobacco, watches, luggage, and pens.

The Vatican Pharmacy, however, is open to all. "People need only tell the guard that they want to enter the Pharmacy, and once inside they must present a medical prescription, just as in any other pharmacy in Rome, and prices are the same,"[23] says Italian journalist Luigi Accattoli, who has covered the Vatican for more than thirty years. The pharmacy was established in 1874, because the Vatican had no medical facilities of its own when it was cut off

Italian firefighters overpower a man who threatened to jump from the dome of St. Peter's Basilica in March 2005.

SPORTS IN THE VATICAN

The Vatican Soccer League actually predates the election of the athletic John Paul II. Since 1970, sixteen teams have played for the annual Vatican Cup. Teams are organized according to where in the Vatican the players work; the maintenance workers, museum staffers, fire department, postal staff, the Swiss Guard, even the secret archives, all have teams. There is even a national team that plays for the Italian amateur championship, reports Luigi Accattoli in his book, *Life in the Vatican with John Paul II*. It goes by the name the Sistine Sporting Group.

Pope John Paul II is presented with a commemorative soccer ball in 1989. The Vatican sponsors its own sixteen-team soccer league.

from the rest of Rome by the establishment of the kingdom of Italy. The facilities were expanded in 1989, and it is presumed that the pharmacy provided the medications given to John Paul II in his last days.

Nearly one hundred people work in the health services of the Vatican. They provide comprehensive health care for residents, as well as emergency first aid for tourists and visitors. Among them are health inspectors, who check the purity of the water supply and the hygiene of the kitchens, restaurants, and the supermarket.

The *sampietrini*—"St. Peter's maintenance men"—is the name for the forty or so men who take care of the cleaning and upkeep of the basilica and the rest of the buildings, as well as the streets and walkways of the city. The *sampietrini's* work is normally behind the scenes, but the chore of maintaining such old, complex, and precious buildings is difficult and expensive. Their colleagues, the *Floreria Apostolica*, build the platforms and install the altars and chairs for large public ceremonies, such as the funeral of John Paul II. On these occasions, the importance of these seemingly mundane jobs is apparent to the world.

Many of these positions have been handed down through working-class Roman families for as long as two centuries. Though this looks rather suspect to American eyes, it is a common and accepted way of doing business in Italy, says an American who has worked in the Vatican for many years. "In America, you're not supposed to hire your relatives," the unidentified source (most people in the Vatican will not allow themselves to be identified in the media) told journalist and priest Thomas Reese. "Here it would be an insult if you didn't. Jobs are passed along. In a way, it works. They know the job better than anyone else. They know everybody. You are not getting somebody you don't know anything about. . . . here, it is like working in a family."[24]

THE VATICAN POST OFFICE

Every day, a thousand letters addressed to the pope arrive in the Vatican Post Office. However, that is just a small fraction of the staggering volume of business it handles—over 4 million outbound letters and 15 million postcards a year. Those numbers are due mainly to tourists who make a point of sending mail home from the Vatican, but many Romans use the Vatican Post Office instead of the notoriously inefficient Italian mail system. Outgoing international mail is flown from the Vatican to Switzerland, where it is sorted and sent on its way.

Vatican postage stamps, which have been issued since 1852, are prized by collectors. They are printed in the Vatican and by a special printery in Switzerland. Almost as sought after is the Vatican postmark, particularly when it reads *Gloria in excelsis Deo*, which is Latin for "Glory to God in the highest."

These Sede Vacante, *or* Vacant See, *stamps were issued in April 2005 after the death of Pope John Paul II and before the election of his successor.*

Most collectible of all are the *Sede Vacante*, or Vacant See, stamps, issued only between the death of one pope and the election of his successor. Following the death of John Paul II in April 2005, the Vatican Post Office issued seven hundred thousand stamps imprinted with the words *Città del Vaticano* and *Sede Vacante MMV* ("Vacant See 2005"). On the stamps, four angels hold a gold canopy over the papal symbol of crossed keys, the canopy hiding the three-tiered-crown above to symbolize the absence of a pope.

VATICAN CURRENCY

Vatican City State coins (there is no paper currency) are in the same denominations as Italian currency and have the same size, weight, and value. They are produced by the Italian Mint. Like Italian currency, Vatican money's value is now pegged to that of the euro, the basic unit of the common currency of the European Union. Vatican coins are still legal tender in Italy and San Marino, and Italian money is legal tender in the Vatican. Like the stamps, Vatican coins are sought by collectors, particularly the coins that are struck to honor specific occasions, such as John Paul II's first visit to Poland in 1979.

VATICAN AUTOMOBILE LICENSES

Even rarer than Vatican stamps or coins are Vatican City license plates, only a few hundred of which exist. Vatican City issues two types of car licenses—official state plates, with the letters SCV (*Stato della Città del Vaticano*), and those for cars belonging to Vatican citizens, with the letters CV (*Città del Vaticano*). Cars reserved for the pope have license plates with red letters on a white background; other plates have black letters on white.

STANDING THE TEST OF TIME

Rarest of all in Vatican City may well be the snap decision. Things are not decided quickly or lightly here. People who have spent time in the Vatican remark on the slow, measured pace of nearly everything that happens there. "In the Vatican, there is always tomorrow," says an American priest in Thomas Reese's book, *Inside the Vatican*. "There is nothing urgent."[25] There is a profound sense of history, as well as a strong perception that what is said or done within those walls is deeply significant and must stand the test of time. The people who live and work inside Vatican City draw daily on two thousand years of faith and tradition to do their jobs.

In Vatican City, even the most mundane tasks have an air of transcendence, an awareness that scrubbing a floor, typing a report, or patching a pothole is special because it is done in service to the pope and God. "In quiet parts of the Vatican," says British journalist George Bull, "one feels not so much a sense of religious revelation as the utter naturalness of acceptance of the supernatural."[26]

THE FUTURE OF
VATICAN CITY

The future of Vatican City is inextricably linked with the future of both the papacy and the Roman Catholic Church. Despite the air of timelessness that pervades the Vatican today, it has seen momentous transformations during its long history. It is only to be expected that the twenty-first century will bring new challenges and changes.

MONEY MATTERS

One pressing matter now, which could be a chronic concern in the future, is money. Though far from financially bankrupt, the Roman Catholic Church is not fabulously wealthy, either. In 2003, the Holy See's accountants reported that the net worth of its patrimony, or real estate holdings, was a relatively modest $908 million. The fact is, the pope controls fewer assets than does the president of Notre Dame University and operates on a budget that is smaller than that of the New York City public school system.

One effect of the Vatican Bank scandal of the 1980s, when millions of dollars of Church assets were invested in questionable, and even illegal, ways, has been a greater openness about Vatican finances. But the veil of secrecy over money matters was not lifted until 1990, when Archbishop Edmund Szoka of Detroit moved to the Vatican to take over the prefecture of economic affairs of the Holy See. He instituted American-style financial oversight, aided by a computer system donated by the American Catholic men's group, the Knights of Columbus. Financial reports for the Holy See and Vatican City State have been issued annually since then. The most recent ones showed that deficit spending, similar to the flood of red ink that plagued the

Holy See between 1970 and 1992, had recurred in the first years of the twenty-first century.

After making small profits for eight years, the Holy See ran deficits in 2001, 2002, and 2003. Income—from investments and contributions—totaled 203.6 million euros. (In 2003, 1 euro was roughly equivalent to 1 U.S. dollar; in 2005, the euro was worth about $1.25.) But expenditures were 213.2 million euros, creating a deficit that equaled about 11.8 million dollars.

Vatican City's budget, which is separate from that of the Holy See, and which historically has shown steady profits, also ran in the red in 2003. Though its income of 145.9 million euros was up 5 percent over 2002's revenues, the city's surplus was tapped for 10.5 million euros to finance Vatican Radio. The cost of maintaining the Vatican's buildings, streets, and city services, as well as paying the 123 members of the Vatican security force and housing the 110 men of the Swiss Guard—all Vatican City responsibilities—went up 15 percent as well. This resulted in a shortfall of 6.8 million euros.

The 2003 annual report belied impressions that contributions to the Holy See by the world's Catholics had declined.

St. Peter's Basilica is one of the best-known landmarks of Vatican City.

THE VATICAN'S SOUP KITCHEN

Like many churches around the world, St. Peter's has a place to feed the hungry. Tucked alongside the Palace of the Holy Office is a small building bearing a sign that reads: "This house is a gift of Mary. Missionaries of Charity." Beside an intercom, a sign in Italian reads: "House of welcome for the poorest." This haven for the poor and hungry was opened in 1988 by John Paul II in honor of Mother Teresa, founder of the Missionaries of Charity. The nuns feed over one hundred people daily and can provide beds for seventy women.

The 49 million euros donated were 5.7 percent more than the previous year. Of this, American Catholics gave about one-third.

The Holy See's losses could be blamed on the same economic conditions that damaged the finances of many nations and individuals. It holds about 1 billion dollars in stocks, bonds, and real estate, holdings that lost 6.9 million euros in 2003. The dollar's decline in value relative to the euro and other world currencies hurt as well. Not only do Americans (and their dollars) account for one-third of the money given to the Holy See every year, Thomas Reese points out that many large foreign donors give in dollars, too. "The [decline in value of the] dollar has really hurt them,"[27] he told Associated Press.

At the same time, expenses have risen. The technology that supports the Vatican's worldwide communications gets more sophisticated and costly each year. The Holy See supports missionary activity around the world and has greatly expanded its diplomatic activities as well. Maintaining a diplomatic presence in 174 countries, as well as delegates or observers to several international bodies such as the UN and the World Health Organization, is costly. However, the Vatican sees all these operations as part of the way to bring its message to the world.

LITERALLY PRICELESS

It is a myth that the Holy See possesses enormous financial reserves, say Church officials and most outside observers.

Being the custodian of many of the world's priceless works of art and architecture is a costly burden and liability, they point out. Caring for the world's largest church is expensive, particularly when it is over five hundred years old and visited by millions of people every year. Conserving and exhibiting the Vatican's thousands of art treasures also takes enormous resources.

Many Vatican treasures, such as the *Pietà*, the *Apollo Belvedere*, and the Sistine Chapel, are valued at 1 euro by Vatican accountants. This reflects the fact that they are truly priceless—they could never be sold. Not only does the Vatican itself have a policy of never selling any of its art, the Italian government can—and does—block the sale and export of anything it deems to be part of Italy's national heritage.

A priest celebrates Mass in the United States. One-third of the money the Holy See is given every year comes from Americans.

Nor can the Holy See draw on the physical or financial assets of any of the 2,864 Catholic dioceses or the 412,886 parishes around the world. Each diocese is financially independent and owns the churches, rectories, schools, and other church-related buildings in its area. In addition, many of the Catholic institutions such as hospitals, orphanages, private schools, colleges, and universities are altogether financially independent.

Even the Peter's Pence, the annual collection taken up around the world, usually on Pentecost Sunday, is supposed to be used only to support the Church's missionary and humanitarian work. In times of tight money, it has been tapped to cover the expenses of the Curia, but even many bishops and cardinals criticized that policy.

For the foreseeable future, the Holy See will have to maximize the income-generating potential of Vatican City, work to improve economic conditions for its millions of members in the developing world so they can contribute financially to

A priest distributes Holy Communion wafers to parishioners after a mass in Vietnam. Today three-fourths of the world's Catholics live in Latin America, Asia, and Africa.

its mission, and rely on the generosity of its wealthiest followers. However, some people both inside and outside the Church believe that more radical measures will have to be adopted to ensure financial stability for the Vatican and even the continued existence of the Church.

New Faces, New Voices

The complexion of the Vatican has visibly altered in the past forty years. Beginning in the reign of Paul VI, a multiculturalism came to the Curia and the College of Cardinals. African, Asian, and Latin American faces began to appear daily in the corridors and streets of Vatican City. Latin gave way to a babble of tongues, and English and Italian began to dominate daily speech.

This trend toward internationalism accelerated rapidly in the Catholic Church as a whole. In 1900, there were 272 million Roman Catholics, the vast majority of them living in Europe. In 2000, there were an estimated 1.1 billion Catholics, three-quarters of whom live in the developing nations of Latin America, Asia, and Africa. Neither the Vatican nor the Church at large will be able to maintain its traditional European orientation much longer. It seems certain to most observers that African drums will someday echo through St. Peter's and Asian Christian art will hang in the museums. More importantly, the world view of the Vatican will shift from that of the rich, industrial parts of the globe to the poor, agrarian, and developing areas.

Indications are that Pope Benedict XVI intends to continue John Paul II's pastoral outreach to the world. In the first weeks of his papacy, the German-born pope made public overtures for better relations with Russia, Vietnam, and particularly, the People's Republic of China. Human rights will continue to dominate the Vatican's dealings with the world's national governments, and there are indications that Benedict intends to continue John Paul II's drive to revive and invigorate the Catholic Church's relations with other Christian denominations as well as believers in other religions.

Outreach such as this requires sensitivity for cultures radically different from the Church's tradition. If these policies also win the Church sizeable numbers of new members in parts of the world where it has not been a large presence, the cultural shift of the Vatican could occur very rapidly.

Observers point to the dramatic effect on the Church that true religious freedom for the Catholics of the People's Republic of China could have. There are approximately 4 million Chinese Catholics who are officially registered members of the so-called patriotic churches, where worship, appointments of clergy, and all activities are controlled by the government and cut off from papal authority. Another estimated 8 million Chinese belong to underground churches, which refuse to accept Communist control of their religion and are said to maintain secret contacts with the Vatican. (The cardinal whom John Paul II elevated in 1996, but did not name, is believed to be Chinese.) If China were to allow real religious freedom, many people believe that there would be 50 million Chinese Catholics in a matter of months. Though they would still be a minority in China itself, the almost-instant addition of millions of new members, in one of the most economically powerful nations in the world, would inevitably draw the eyes of the Vatican eastward—and new Chinese bishops, priests, and cardinals to Rome.

A POPE NOT FROM EUROPE?

The effects of this geographic and cultural shift were seen publicly during the funeral of John Paul II and in the conclave of cardinals that chose his successor. The faces of the cardinals arrayed around the altar showed the racial and ethnic diversity that has risen in the Church in the past forty years.

An even more dramatic portent for the future was the lists of *papabile*, the cardinals seen to have a chance of being pope. The lists varied, but every one included the Nigerian Francis Arinze. If Arinze ever does become pope, he would not only be the first black African pope (there were some popes from northern Africa during the Roman era, but the last one, Gelasius I, died in 496), but the first pope to be a convert from a pagan religion since the time of Constantine. (Arinze's family practiced a traditional Ibo animist religion; he converted to Catholicism at age nine.) Though conservative and orthodox in his views of Catholic doctrine, "Arinze has been a strong proponent of efforts to develop a style of Christianity in Africa that reflects African culture rather than the culture of the historically-dominant West," says the Reverend Clarence Williams, director for black Catholic ministries for the Archdiocese of Detroit. "This push goes hand

in hand with anti-colonial sentiment driving political change in Africa."[28] It also harks back to John Paul II's belief that part of basic human rights is that people must be allowed to be true to their culture—and that culturally-driven change can be lasting.

Nigerian Francis Arinze (right) has worked to develop a style of Christianity that reflects African rather than European culture.

Other *papabile* in 2005 were Honduran Oscar Rodriquez Maradiaga, Brazilian Claudio Hummes, Mexican Norberto Carrera, and Ivan Dias, ethnically Portuguese but Indian-born, who is Archbishop of Bombay. Even though all these men are doctrinally conservative in the mold of John Paul II, who elevated each of them to cardinal, each of them, if elected pope, would bring a different worldview to the papacy.

BLACK SMOKE/WHITE SMOKE— HOW A POPE IS ELECTED

Sworn to secrecy and isolated in the Sistine Chapel and the Domum St. Martha, 120 cardinals under age eighty elect a pope. To vote, each cardinal receives a ballot bearing the words "*Eligo in suumum pontificem*—I elect as supreme pontiff . . . " on which he writes a name. The cardinal folds his ballot and places it on a small gold plate called a paten, which rests atop a chalice on the altar. He then lifts the paten, slides the ballot into the chalice, replaces the paten on top of the chalice, and returns to his seat. When all the votes are cast, the dean of the College of Cardinals counts the ballots aloud. If no one receives more than two-thirds of the vote, the ballots are burned in a stove with a chemical added that makes the smoke black. Black smoke tells the crowd assembled in St. Peter's Square that no pope has been elected.

After thirty inconclusive votes, new rules say the cardinals may elect a pope by a simple majority, that is, half the votes plus one. Some fear that this could discourage the kind of compromise elections that have occurred in the past.

This possibility remains to be seen. What is certain is that when the next pope is elected, the first public sign will be the traditional puffs of white smoke as the ballots that elected him are burned, unadulterated, in the Sistine Chapel stove.

Black smoke billowing from a chimney at the Sistine Chapel signifies that a new pope has not yet been elected.

RADICAL PROPOSALS FOR REFORM

Many people inside the Catholic Church believe that the only way it will flourish in the coming century is if it decentralizes. The Second Vatican Council adopted several documents calling for more collegiality in the Church, that is to say, more sharing of power among the bishops and less authority centralized in the Vatican. Exactly the opposite happened during the long reign of John Paul II. Because of his dynamic personality and his traditional, authoritarian views, John Paul II actually increased both the power of the pope and the authority of the Curia. In the view of some theologians and Church leaders, the Church is back to where it was sixty years ago, with every decision made in Rome. In the view of other theologians and Church leaders, including Pope Benedict XVI, that is exactly how it should be.

Some Catholics who are unhappy with that state of affairs believe that collegiality will not happen unless the Curia is abolished. They point out that it is not a very old institution, in the Vatican scheme of things, dating only to the seventeenth century. They believe that a restructuring of Church leadership to resemble the way it was before the popes became secular rulers as well as spiritual ones will restore the bishops to their historical (and they believe, correct) positions of authority in the Church. An Australian theologian, Paul Collins, says the Curia should be set aside in favor of a small secretariat for papal affairs. Then bishops could make ecclesiastical decisions in an atmosphere of cooperation and openness.

A few of these reform-minded Catholics also believe that the long papacy of John Paul II has shown the need for term limits for popes. At a meeting of the international Catholic group We Are Church in Rome shortly before the 2005 conclave, Sri Lankan theologian Tissa Balisuriya suggested papal reigns should last no more than ten years. This, he argues, would safeguard the church from papal personality cults fueled by the media age. We must not "make the pope God,"[29] he said.

Others at the conference urged a new Ecumenical Council to look at the nature of the Church itself in the fast-changing modern world. A new council, they said, should be held outside of Rome, as most councils in the past were—a signal to the world of the Church's independence from both Western domination and the Roman Curia.

Pope Benedict XVI waves to the crowd at St. Peter's Basilica. Even with proposals to decentralize its power, Vatican City is likely to remain the heart of the Catholic Church for a long time to come.

STAYING POWER

Radical change is unlikely to come to the Vatican anytime soon. In a place like the Vatican, and an institution like the Catholic Church, both of which measure their life spans in millennia, change is usually very deliberate and very slow. Even issues that have nothing to do with doctrine or belief are studied minutely and prayed over before any decisions are made. Apart from an ingrained reluctance to change anything that could affect the spiritual lives of the faithful, the people inside the Vatican can marshal many arguments against altering the current way of doing things.

For example, abolishing the Curia would greatly reduce the Vatican's operating costs, because, like any institution or corporation, personnel costs are its largest expense. But doing so would also put nearly two thousand lay Romans out of work, which would not only be unfair, but would cause a major public relations problem for the Church in Italy. A decentralized Church would rely even more than it does now on communications; more financial resources will have to be put into the technology that makes it possible. Though there are many prominent theologians and Church leaders who believe that decentralization is more in line with the earliest organization of the Church, there are other equally prominent theologians and leaders, Pope Benedict XVI among them, who firmly believe that the Church's universality and mission to reach all people require top-down, centralized authority.

Even if the Curia were gone and the leadership of the Church equally ensconced in Singapore, Nairobi, São Paulo, and Toronto, the Vatican would still be one of the world's great spiritual centers. Pilgrims would still flock to the tomb of St. Peter and pack Masses on holy days. No matter how secular the postindustrial world becomes, its affluent citizens will still flock to see the masterpieces of the Vatican Museums, the stirring ceiling of the Sistine Chapel, and the soaring dome of St. Peter's. The Church can no more sell off the art and close the Vatican than U.S. leaders could board up Independence Hall.

"The salvation of souls and the future of humankind will be influenced by decisions made inside the Vatican,"[30] says Thomas Reese. Even if more authority to govern the Church is spread out among the bishops and the size of the bureaucracy reduced, Vatican City will still be the center of the Catholic Church. Peter's bones beneath the high altar and the presence of his papal successor will guarantee it.

FACTS ABOUT VATICAN CITY

GENERAL INFORMATION

Official name: State of the City of the Vatican (the Holy See)

Type of government: Theocracy with an elected sovereign; electorate limited to members of the College of Cardinals under the age of eighty, who can elect only a Catholic male to be pope

Chief of state: Pope Benedict XVI

Head of government: Secretary of State Cardinal Angelo Sodano

Official language: Latin

Other languages: Italian, English

Legal system: Based on Code of Canon Law

Constitution: Fundamental Law, revised 1998

Monetary unit: Vatican lire

Exchange rate: Tied to Italian currency (still in use) and the euro

Area: 0.2 sq. mi (0.44 sq. km)

PEOPLE

Population: (2005) 921

Population growth: (2005) 0.01 percent

Demographics: 98 percent male, 2 percent female, average age 60+

Religion: Roman Catholic

Voting: Limited to members of the College of Cardinals under the age of eighty; no other citizens have the vote

ECONOMY

Revenues: $245.2 million

Expenditures: (2002) $260.4 million

Industries: Tourism; printing, production of coins, medals, postage stamps, and mosaics

Radio stations: Two AM, four FM, two shortwave

Television stations: One

Newspaper: One daily

SUPERLATIVES

Smallest nation in the world in terms of both geographic size and population

Only entire nation to be named a UN International Heritage Site

Site of the world's largest church, St. Peter's Basilica

Defended by the world's smallest and oldest armed force, the Swiss Guard

NOTES

CHAPTER 1: THE GREATEST MUSEUM IN THE WORLD

1. Luigi Accattoli, *Life in the Vatican with John Paul II*. New York: Universe, 1998, p. 93.

CHAPTER 2: THE HISTORY OF VATICAN CITY

2. Christopher Hibbert, *Rome: The Biography of a City*. London: Penguin, 1985, p. 341.

3. Hibbert, *Rome*, p. 344.

4. Quoted in Hibbert, *Rome*, p. 230.

5. Quoted in Hibbert, *Rome*, p. 303.

CHAPTER 3: THE GLORY AND THE POWER

6. Thomas Reese, S.J., *Inside the Vatican*. Cambridge, MA: Harvard University Press, 1996, p. 23.

7. George Bull, *Inside the Vatican.* New York: St. Martin's, 1982, p. 75.

8. Reverend Edward Domin, personal interview with the author, April 27, 2005.

9. Domin interview.

10. John L. Allen Jr., *All the Pope's Men*. New York: Doubleday, 2004, p. 189.

11. Reese, *Inside the Vatican*, p. 106.

12. Reese, *Inside the Vatican*, p. 125.

CHAPTER 4: THE WORLD'S SMALLEST SUPERPOWER

13. Allen, *All the Pope's Men*, p. 149.

14. Allen, *All the Pope's Men*, p. 47.

15. George Weigel, "Pope John Paul II and the Dynamics of History," Foreign Policy Research Institute, April 2000. www.fpri.org/ww/0106.200004.weigel.popehistory.html.

16. Weigel, "Pope John Paul II and the Dynamics of History."

17. Mark Laudy, "The Vatican Mediation of the Beagle Channel Dispute: Crisis Intervention and Forum Building," in *Words over War: Mediation and Arbitration to Prevent Deadly Conflict*, eds. Melanie Greenberg, et al. New York: Carnegie, 2001, pp. 304–305.

18. Weigel, "Pope John Paul II and the Dynamics of History."

Chapter 5: Everyday Life in Vatican City

19. Bull, *Inside the Vatican*, pp. 163, 166.

20. Quoted in Cindy Wooden, "For Ailing Pope, a Picture Is Worth a Thousand Words, Jesuit Says," Catholic News Service, March 24, 2005. www.catholicnews.com.

21. Quoted in Accattoli, *Life in the Vatican with John Paul II*, p. 209.

22. Reese, *Inside the Vatican*, p. 21.

23. Accattoli, *Life in the Vatican with John Paul II*, p. 195.

24. Quoted in Reese, *Inside the Vatican*, p. 154.

25. Quoted in Reese, *Inside the Vatican*, p. 161.

26. Bull, *Inside the Vatican*, p. 75.

Chapter 6: The Future of Vatican City

27. Quoted in Victor L. Simpson, "Vatican Finances Will Need Shepherd," *Morning Call*, April 15, 2005, p. A3.

28. Clarence Williams, "White Smoke for a Black Pope?" Beliefnet, October 2000. www.beliefnet.com/story/48/story_4829/html.

29. Quoted in Joan Chittiser, "Never Mind the Papabile, Consider the Papacy," *National Catholic Reporter*, April 17, 2005. NCRonline.org.

30. Reese, *Inside the Vatican*, p. 8.

CHRONOLOGY

A.D. 66
Apostle Peter is martyred in the circus on Vatican Hill, near Caligula's obelisk; he is buried in a nearby cemetery, and his tomb becomes a Christian shrine.

313–320
Emperor Constantine legalizes the practice of Christianity and converts, moves the seat of government of the Roman Empire east to Constantinople but starts construction of a great basilica in honor of Peter on the site of the shrine, donates Lateran Palace as a residence for the pope, and constructs the Basilica of St. John Lateran.

400–600
Rome is attacked and sacked repeatedly by barbarian tribes.

CA. 500
Pope Symmachus builds a residence alongside St. Peter's.

753
Papal States are established.

800
Charlemagne is crowned Holy Roman Emperor in St. Peter's on Christmas Day.

847–853
Rome is sacked again; Pope Leo IV builds walls and fortifications around St. Peter's and its surroundings, enclosing the area for the first time that later becomes the Vatican.

1305
Pope Clement V moves to Avignon, France, under the orders of the French king; the so-called Avignon Papacy lasts sixty-seven years, but the controversy over who was the rightful pope continues until 1414, a period known as the Great Schism.

September 1348
Severe earthquakes strike Rome, damaging St. Peter's, the
Lateran Palace, the Basilica of St. John Lateran, and ancient
buildings, including the Colosseum.

CA. 1450
Pope Nicholas V decides to replace the old St. Peter's with a
larger, grander, domed cathedral and names Leon Alberti
as architect for a new basilica.

1475–1481
The Sistine Chapel is built and partially decorated by Sandro Botticelli.

1503–1513
Pope Julius II demolishes the old St. Peter's and hires Donato Bramante to design and build a new basilica, commissions Michelangelo to paint the ceiling of the Sistine
Chapel, creates the first formal Vatican Gardens, and moves
his private art collection to the Vatican.

1574
Pope Gregory XIII builds the Quirinal Palace in an area of
Rome believed to be healthier than the Lateran Palace; the
Quirinal is used continuously as the papal residence from
the reign of Clement VIII (1592–1605) until the fall of
Rome to the Italians in 1870, when Pius IX retreats to
the Vatican.

1590
The dome of St. Peter's is completed, topped with a cross,
and dedicated; the Papal Palace, also known as the Apostolic Palace, which now contains the private apartments of
the pope, is also completed.

1610
Pope Paul V commissions Carlo Maderna to finish the nave
of St. Peter's.

1656–1667
Gian Lorenzo Bernini designs and builds St. Peter's Square
and the colonnade, commissioned by Pope Alexander VII.

1770–1795
Clement XIV commissions the building of the first Vatican gallery for art and sculpture; by the time the building is completed, in the reign of Pius VI, it is too small; Pius doubles the size of the Clementine Museum, which becomes known as the Pio-Clementine Museum.

1798
Napoleon occupies Rome, sends Pius VI into exile, where he dies, and loots the Vatican of its art treasures.

1808
Napoleon formally annexes the Papal States and is excommunicated by Pius VII; in retaliation, Napoleon strips the pope of temporal rule and exiles him.

1816
The Congress of Vienna restores the Papal States and orders the looted art treasures returned to Rome.

1860
The Papal States of Romagna, Umbria, and Marche vote to join the new Italian kingdom.

1870
Rome falls to Italian armies; King Victor Emmanuel II moves into the Quirinal Palace; Pope Pius IX retreats to the Vatican, denounces the new nation as invalid, forbids Catholics from any participation, including voting, in the new nation, and proclaims himself the "prisoner of the Vatican."

1929
The Lateran Treaty is signed between Pope Pius XI and King Victor Emmanuel III of Italy; the State of the City of the Vatican is recognized as a sovereign nation, giving the pope legal status under international law as a head of state.

1931
Pope Pius XI asks Guglielmo Marconi, the inventor of radio, to install a radio station and transmitter in the Vatican Gardens.

1939–1945
Pope Pius XII declares the Vatican officially neutral in World War II and opens the Vatican to refugees from all over

Europe; during food shortages late in the war, the Vatican feeds as many as one hundred thousand Romans a day.

1962
Pope John XXIII convenes the Second Vatican Council and calls for a "new wind" to blow through the Vatican and the Catholic Church; significant changes in Catholic liturgies result, including the switch from Latin to vernacular languages.

1963
John XXIII dies and is succeeded by Pope Paul VI, who becomes the first pope to travel outside Italy and to visit the United States.

1978
Cardinal Karol Wojtyla is elected pope to succeed John Paul I, whose reign lasted only 33 days; John Paul II, the youngest pope in over 130 years and the first non-Italian pope in over 400 years, travels over 600,000 miles (966,000km) during his reign, which is also marked by the opening of a Vatican television station and Internet communications.

April 2005
John Paul II dies at age eighty-four; over 1 million people wait for days to view his body and attend his funeral; Pope Benedict XVI, formerly Cardinal Joseph Ratzinger, is elected.

FOR FURTHER READING

BOOKS

Helen Becker and Susan Grimbly, *The Everything Catholicism Book*. Avon, MA: Adams Media, 2003. Easy to read and broken down into blocks of straightforward information that help the reader understand the Catholic Church and its beliefs and practices.

Judith Cozzens and the Young Writers Workshop, *Kids Explore America's Catholic Heritage*. Denver: Pauline Books and Media, 2002. Researched, written, and illustrated by over one hundred Catholic kids from third to seventh grades, covering the history of Catholicism in America, American saints, the Mass, and basic Catholic doctrine.

William Lace, *The Vatican*, San Diego: Lucent, 2003. This book traces the origins and physical growth of the ruling center of the Catholic Church.

Renee Rebman, *The Sistine Chapel*. San Diego: Lucent, 2000. The author focuses on the epic of Michelangelo's ceiling and its twentieth-century restoration.

Reverend John Triglio and Reverend Kenneth Brighanti, *Catholicism for Dummies*. Indianapolis: Wiley, 2003. The popular Dummies format applied to Catholic history, canon law, doctrines, and theology, by two priests associated with the Eternal Word Television Network.

WEB SITES

Inside the Vatican: National Geographic Goes Behind the Public Facade, National Geographic Society News (http://

news.nationalgeographic.com/news./2001/11/118_
vaticanmain.html). Text and photos from a National Geographic television special on the Vatican.

Vatican Museums (mv.vatican.va). This sophisticated Web
site, dedicated to the museums, allows virtual tours of
several of the Vatican Museums.

Vatican Radio (www.vaticanradio.org). Schedules, program
listings, and live and taped broadcasts that can be heard
online in thirty-five languages.

WORKS CONSULTED

BOOKS

Luigi Accattoli, *Life in the Vatican with John Paul II*. New York: Universe, 1998. Vatican-authorized and heavily illustrated with beautiful photos, this book combines an insider tour of Vatican City with an intimate account of the daily life of the pope and other residents of the Vatican.

John L. Allen Jr., *All the Pope's Men*. New York: Doubleday, 2004. A balanced, lively, insider's look at the operations, sociology, and anthropology of the Vatican and its relationship with the Catholic Church in the United States. The author is an American journalist who is the Vatican correspondent for the *National Catholic Reporter* and a Vatican analyst for CNN and NPR.

Maurice Andrieux, *Daily Life in Papal Rome*. London: George Allen and Unwin, 1968. A scholarly account, full of fascinating details, of Roman life under the benevolent rule of the eighteenth-century popes.

Carl Bernstein and Marco Politi, *His Holiness: John Paul II and the Hidden History of Our Time*. New York: Doubleday, 1996. This biography of the Polish pope, with a focus on his role in the end of the Cold War and the collapse of European communism, is by one of the United States's most famous investigative reporters and the dean of the Italian press corps in the Vatican.

George Bull, *Inside the Vatican*. New York: St. Martin's, 1982. Written by a leading British journalist and Renaissance literature translator, this is a sympathetic, but not fawning, look at the early years of the reign of John Paul II and how the Polish papacy shifted operations and some outlooks in the Vatican.

Redig de Campos, ed., *Art Treasures of the Vatican*. London: Park Lane, 1974. Large format book with over four hundred color images of sculptures, paintings, tapestries, mosaics, frescoes, and antiquities in the Vatican, with explanatory footnotes.

Robert I.C. Fisher, *Fodor's Holy Rome*. New York: Fodor's Travel Publications, 1999. Concise but detailed descriptions of sites in Vatican City, as well as the rest of Rome, with essays explaining the history and significance of each.

Christopher Hibbert, *Rome: The Biography of a City*. London: Penguin, 1985. Scholarly, detailed, and lively history of the Eternal City, the life and times of which have been indivisibly yoked with that of the Vatican, the popes, and the Roman Catholic Church for nearly two thousand years.

Carl Koch, *A Popular History of the Catholic Church*. Winona, MN: St. Mary's, 1997. Concise, factual history of the Roman Catholic Church.

Mark Laudy, "The Vatican Mediation of the Beagle Channel Dispute: Crisis Intervention and Forum Building," in *Words over War: Mediation and Arbitration to Prevent Deadly Conflict*, eds. Melanie Greenberg, et al. New York: Carnegie, 2001.

Malachi Martin, *Rich Church, Poor Church*. New York: G.P. Putnam's Sons, 1984. A discussion of Vatican finances in the context of the banking scandal of the 1980s.

Metropolitan Museum of Art, *The Vatican Collections: The Papacy and Art*. New York: Abrams, 1982. The official catalog of the exhibit of the same name, officially authorized by the Vatican Museums, for an exhibit of 237 works of art mounted in 1982. Includes detailed interpretive descriptions of each work, including the history and provenance.

Bart McDowell, *Inside the Vatican*. Washington, DC: National Geographic Society, 1991. Stunning photographs and illustrations outshine the relatively short and simple text of this classic National Geographic book. Especially notable are the cutaway drawing of St. Peter's and the diagram that overlays the Roman circus, the original basilica, the necropolis, and the current building, and color-codes of the present St. Peter's according to the designs of its various architects.

Thomas J. Reese, S.J., *Inside the Vatican.* Cambridge, MA: Harvard University Press, 1996. Reese is a political scientist, sociologist, and theologian who brings scholarly analysis as well as theological insight to the inner workings of the Holy See.

PERIODICALS

Ian Fisher and Laurie Goodstein, "Benedict XVI Is Installed as 265th Pope at Outdoor Mass," *New York Times*, April 25, 2005.

Tami A. Quigley, "Vatican Organist Inspires Capacity Crowd at Concert in Bethlehem," *AD Times*, September 19, 1996.

Victor L. Simpson, "Vatican Finances Will Need Shepherd," *Morning Call*, April 15, 2005.

INTERNET SOURCES

Associated Press, "Pope Benedict XVI Gets E-mail Address," MSNBC.com. April 21, 2005. www.msnbc.com/id/7587388.

Matthew Bunson, "Talking to Your Kids About the Vatican," Our Sunday Visitor, May 1, 1999. www.osv.com/periodicals/show-article.asp?pid=534.

Joan Chittiser, "Never Mind the Papabile, Consider the Papacy," National Catholic Reporter, April 17, 2005. NCRonline.org.

Daniel Engber, "Is the Conclave Held in Latin?" Slate.com, April 7, 2005. www.slate.com.

Betsy Hiel, "'Vacant See' at Post Office," PittsburgLIVE.com, April 26, 2005. http://pittsburghlive.com/x/tribune-review/s_323517.html.

George Weigel, "Pope John Paul II and the Dynamics of

History," Foreign Policy Research Institute, April 2000. www.fpri.org/ww/0106.20004.weigel.popehistory.html.

Clarence Williams, "White Smoke for a Black Pope?" Beliefnet, October 2000. www.beliefnet.com/story/48/story_4829/html.

Cindy Wooden, "For Ailing Pope, a Picture Is Worth a Thousand Words, Jesuit Says," Catholic News Service, March 24, 2005. www.catholicnews.com.

WEB SITES

The Art of Fresco (www.muralist.org/fresco). Web site of American organization dedicated to fresco painting.

The Christian Catacombs of Rome (www.catacombe.roma. it). History and tourist information on the Catacombs.

CIA World Factbook 2005 (www.cia.gov). Statistical information about Vatican City, including geography, economics, and demographics.

National Catholic Reporter (www.natcath.com). Online version of the weekly independent U.S. newspaper.

The Official Website of the Holy See/Vatican City (www. vatican.va). Official news, the pope's calendar, events, and extensive background information on the Holy See, Vatican City, and the Roman Catholic Church.

Right or Wrong? The Restoration of the Sistine Chapel (www.arches.uga.edu/~msopa129/htm). Analysis of the pros and cons of the restoration, with before-and-after photos.

Vatican Museums (http://mv.vatican.va). Information and virtual tours of Vatican art collections.

INDEX

PICTURE CREDITS

ABOUT THE AUTHOR

Martha Capwell Fox, who sang Gregorian chant in Latin in her grade school choir, is a freelance writer and editor in Catasauqua, Pennsylvania. She has written extensively about nutrition and health, as well as about the histories of swimming, auto racing, and the silk industry.